GCSE
Leisure & Tourism

Stephen Rick

Philip Allan Updates
Market Place
Deddington
Oxfordshire
OX15 0SE

tel: 01869 338652
fax: 01869 337590
e-mail: sales@philipallan.co.uk
www.philipallan.co.uk

ISBN-13: 978-1-84489-406-2
ISBN-10: 1-84489-406-1

Author's acknowledgements
Thanks as always to Debbie and Katie and to Philip Cross and all at Philip Allan as well as to Clare for her support and interest.

Illustrations by Dylan Gibson.
Printed in Great Britain by CPI Bath.

Environmental information
The paper on which this title is printed is sourced from managed, sustainable forests.

P00642

Contents

Introduction iv

Topic 1 The leisure and tourism industries

1.1 The leisure industry 2

1.2 National leisure facilities 18

1.3 Visitor attractions 28

1.4 Home-based leisure and leisure-time choices 38

1.5 The travel and tourism industry 43

1.6 UK tourism destinations 56

1.7 Combining leisure and tourism 66

Topic 2 Marketing in leisure and tourism

2.1 What is marketing? 76

2.2 The marketing mix 87

2.3 SWOT analysis 103

2.4 Building your marketing portfolio 108

Topic 3 Customer service in leisure and tourism

3.1 Customers 116

3.2 Dealing with customers 126

3.3 Customer complaints and records 136

3.4 Building your customer-service portfolio 141

Index 148

Introduction

This textbook has been written to support your learning in the three units that make up the AQA Double Award GCSE in Leisure and Tourism. It provides comprehensive coverage of the unit content laid down by the AQA specifications. It can also be used to help support the learning of GCSE Leisure and Tourism students following the OCR, Edexcel, WJEC and CEA specifications. The *AQA GCSE Leisure and Tourism Student Workbook*, also written by Stephen Rickerby and published by Philip Allan Updates, accompanies this textbook.

Course structure

Unit 1 is an externally assessed unit (it has an examination), but Units 2 and 3 are both internally assessed (coursework) units for which you need to produce your own work as evidence of your achievements.

In this textbook, Topic 1 provides the key knowledge and understanding needed for the examination, as well as helping build the appropriate skills, including description, explanation, analysis and evaluation. Topics 2 and 3 cover coursework and are intended to assess your learning of the relevant study areas. This textbook provides the information that you will need to help you build the knowledge, understanding and skills necessary to complete your coursework.

Assessment objectives

Throughout your work for all three units, you will acquire and apply knowledge, understanding and skills (including investigation skills). You will be assessed against three assessment objectives (AOs):
- show knowledge and understanding (AO1)
- apply knowledge, skills and understanding (AO2)
- plan and carry out investigations and evaluate evidence (AO3)

This book provides learning material to help you demonstrate achievement against the three assessment objectives in the Unit 1 examination and in your coursework for Units 2 and 3.

Special features of this book

A holistic view

The leisure and tourism industries form a single subject for study. Although the course is split into three discrete assessment units (as reflected by some teaching methods), your understanding of the subject will be greatly enhanced by a realisation that the industries introduced in Topic 1 ('The leisure and tourism industries') are the same as those whose marketing and customer-service provision are the subjects of Topics 2 and 3 ('Marketing leisure and tourism' and 'Customer service in leisure and tourism').

This book and its accompanying workbook recognise the holistic nature of leisure and tourism. They provide opportunities for under-standing and activities that cross the boundaries between units, so that you build awareness of the subject as a whole.

Case studies

Real leisure and tourism organisations, facilities and destinations are the subjects of case studies that help to increase your knowledge and understanding of the leisure and tourism industry. Case studies in this book are up to date at the time of publication.

Knowledge of case studies is vital for scoring higher marks in the examination. Longer answers are marked according to two or three levels of response. The upper half of the marks available for longer answers are typically at Level 2. In order to reach Level 2 in the examination, you must show clear application of knowledge, under-standing and skills. Often this means showing sufficient knowledge of leisure and tourism facilities, organisations and destinations to be able to convey a real sense of place. The examiner should be given the impression that you have a real knowledge and understanding of the examples you use. Learning case studies is thus essential if you aspire to a higher grade (C and above).

Case studies provide a base of learning from which you can launch your own investigations for the two coursework units. It is essential that you have a good grasp of the marketing and customer service topics before beginning to investigate and assemble your own portfolios.

The range of case studies in this textbook is wide. They include facilities, organisations and destinations from major players to the small to medium-sized enterprises that are so important to the leisure and tourism industries. Examples from the public, private and voluntary sectors of the economy are used. UK destinations that

appeal to domestic, outbound and inbound tourists from the UK, Europe and wider world are showcased.

Have a go

At the end of each chapter, and within many of them, menus of activities are presented in three columns. In each column, at least one learning activity is proposed to support your work towards each of the three assessment objectives. There is one column per assessment objective, so column 1 is for AO1, column 2 for AO2 and the final column for AO3.

The *AQA GCSE Leisure and Tourism Student Workbook* is a source of additional stimulus-led activities to support achievement.

Practical scenarios

These feature in each topic. They are extended practical activities that guide you to research real leisure and tourism industry organisations and places. They build learning for the examination and act as platforms underpinning more detailed investigation for your coursework units. In Topics 2 and 3, the practical scenarios are activities that build knowledge, understanding and skills before you embark on your own coursework portfolio.

Course advice

General advice

- Keep up to date. There are two dimensions to this:
  Your own work: there is a lot to learn and do in the time your course lasts, so it is important from the start to stay on schedule with tasks you are set and with your portfolio work. Make a written or electronic schedule and monitor yourself. If minor deviations occur, you can reschedule, but try not to fall too far behind. If there is a problem, ask your teacher for advice.
  The changing world of leisure and tourism: this book is as up to date as possible. However, the leisure and tourism industries and the real world in which they operate are constantly changing. Use the media to keep up to date with this changing world. Information sources, including some websites, are suggested in this book as tools to help you.
- Read this book selectively and in bite-size chunks to support your learning in tandem with the teaching you receive.
- Know and understand the case studies. For the examination, these provide valuable knowledge that you can use to help you score more marks. In particular, for Level 2 marks you need to show that you know about real leisure and tourism facilities, organisations

and places. For Units 2 and 3, the case studies provide you with important insights that you can apply to your investigations.

■ Practise and develop your skills, including description, explanation, analysis and evaluation. The 'Have a go' menu at the end of each chapter provides you with appropriate opportunities.

Examination advice

■ Read each question carefully. Every word in the question will have been chosen intentionally by the examiner, so make sure that you read and consider the meaning of every word. Focus on the key words.

■ Obey the command words. The command word in a question is the instructing word. 'Name', 'outline', 'describe', 'suggest', 'explain', 'compare' and 'justify' are some common command words. Meanings for these and others are as follows:

Name: write what something, someone or somewhere is called. Often, a single word or two is all that is needed.

Outline: use sentences to give just the main points that are needed to make clear that you know and understand something.

Describe: write an account of the main features of something in a little more detail using adjectives. There is no need to explain.

Suggest reasons for: briefly identify why something is as it is; usually a number of reasons will be specified by the question.

Explain: use sentences to clarify why something is as it is, using linking words such as 'because' and 'so'.

Analyse: show you understand some statistics or links in depth by using sentences to break down a subject into its essential elements and explain how they affect each other and their causes. Come to a conclusion.

Evaluate: weigh up the issue, giving strengths and weaknesses. Write sentences to assess extent (how much?), likelihood (what are the chances of?) or significance (how important?)

Justify: use sentences to make clear the reasons behind a decision you have reached or a recommendation you have made.

■ Practise examination-type questions including past papers published by AQA, as well as those in the 'Have a go' menu at the end of each chapter and in the *AQA GCSE Leisure and Tourism Student Workbook*.

■ Stick to the point in your answers to the questions. Refer back to the question wording to ensure that you both satisfy its instruction and avoid irrelevance. Make use of appropriate case-study knowledge to illustrate your points.

■ Revise thoroughly.

Coursework advice

- Remember that your portfolios are assessments of what you know, understand and are able to do.
- Learn and understand underpinning theoretical knowledge first. This includes learning and practising the application of your knowledge and understanding to case-study examples of real leisure and tourism industry organisations or destinations.
- Make use of this book and the *AQA GCSE Leisure and Tourism Student Workbook*, as well as the 'Have a go' sections.
- Take particular note of Chapters 2.4 and 3.4 when building your portfolio.
- You should have acquired the knowledge, understanding and skills needed for at least the first assessment task that you are set before embarking upon it.
- Develop, improve and practise the required skills, such as customer-service skills, before they are assessed.
- Complete one assessment task at a time to build your portfolio for Units 2 and 3.
- Give proof of your research by quoting the sources you have used. It is good practice to identify each source in any text you produce and cross-reference it with a list of sources. For example, if you have used some figures from the Statistics on Tourism and Research UK website (**www.staruk.org.uk**), you should name the source next to the figures you took from it and quote it again in a references section at the end of your portfolio. If quoting from this book, you could refer to it in brackets after the quotation in the format '(Rickerby 2006)' and then give fuller details in the references section: 'Rickerby, S. (2006) *AQA GCSE Leisure and Tourism*, Philip Allan Updates'.
- Meet deadlines you have agreed or have been set. Consider breaking down an assessment task into several parts and plan mini-deadlines for each.
- Follow carefully the wording for each assessment task and ensure you do exactly what it says. Make sure you understand what the wording requires at different levels of achievement.
- Aim high.
- Act on feedback to ensure success at your target level of achievement.

Topic 1

The leisure and tourism industries

Chapter

1.1

The leisure industry

Leisure activities

People take part in leisure activities in their spare time. They are activities that people enjoy when they are not working — work is the opposite of leisure. Sleeping does not count as leisure, because during sleep people are not consciously engaged in an activity. Leisure activities involve people when they are awake and not working — they are activities that allow people to relax and enjoy themselves.

There are many leisure activities, including playing or watching any sport. Other ways to spend leisure time include:

- reading a book or magazine
- going out for any form of entertainment (to a cinema, theatre, nightclub or bowling alley)
- going for a run or walking the dog
- playing a computer game, watching the television or listening to CDs or the radio
- taking part in exercise, e.g. going to the gym or a swimming pool
- playing games such as chess, snooker, cards or dominoes
- solving crosswords and sudoku puzzles

▼ *Figure 1.1*
Some leisure
activities

- having adventures like whitewater rafting or hot-air ballooning
- visiting tourist attractions such as Blackpool Tower, Stonehenge, Madame Tussaud's wax museum or the National Gallery in London

Figure 1.1 shows a range of leisure activities and Figure 1.2 suggests how someone might spend a day of leisure.

Some people think of shopping as leisure. Going shopping, perhaps with a group of friends, can be fun. However, buying essentials such as food and clothes to keep warm and dry is not formally classified as a leisure activity. This is because shopping for essentials is something that people do in order to live. Leisure is enjoyment beyond what we need to do just to survive.

Leisure activities are supported by the leisure industry. It is made up of the huge set of organisations that provide the products and services that people want for their leisure activities. Products are the objects that customers want to buy, rent or borrow. Services are what people in an organisation do for their customers. The retail industry includes shops, which are not part of the leisure industry.

Figure 1.3 shows a multiplex cinema, which has several screens that show different films. Companies that own cinemas provide products and services for their customers' leisure. The cinema offers the experience of watching a film. This is the main product that the customers buy. Employees at the cinema sell tickets to the customers and guide them to the correct seating area. These are both services. In addition, there is often a catering service selling products such as popcorn and fizzy drinks.

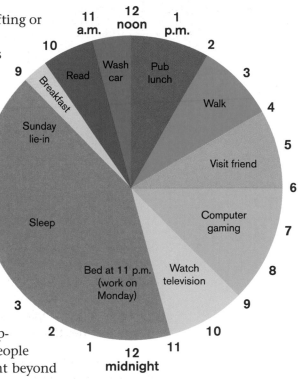

▲ *Figure 1.2*
A leisure day: one person's Sunday

▲ *Figure 1.3 A multiplex cinema*

Publishing Pictures

α 3

Behind-the-scenes services are those that the customer does not see because they are usually hidden from view. In the multiplex cinema shown in Figure 1.3, services such as cleaning, maintenance and projecting the films take place behind the scenes.

Have a Go

Know and understand	Apply what you know	Investigate
1 a Make a poster to illustrate your own leisure activities.	**2 a** Describe the leisure day shown in Figure 1.2.	**3 a** Investigate the leisure activities of people in your class and their families.
b Explain, using examples, what leisure is and what it is not.	**b** Draw leisure-day pie charts for: ● yourself ● someone much older	Compile a questionnaire and use graphs to present the results.
	c Compare your leisure day with that of an older person.	**b** Assess how age and gender affect the leisure activities of different people.

✓Key components of the leisure industry

Components are parts that are put together to make up something bigger. The leisure industry is made up of components. The parts that are important are **key components**. In the leisure industry there are seven key components:

- sport and physical recreation
- arts and entertainment
- countryside recreation
- home-based leisure
- children's play activities
- visitor attractions
- catering

Sport and physical recreation include participation in any sport — indoor or outdoor — such as football, horse racing, basketball or squash. Sport is competitive, but physical recreation is having fun in a way that makes demands on the body (often with the intention of keeping fit) without necessarily being competitive. Using fitness equipment in a gym is physical recreation without being sport. Running is a sport (athletics) if it involves participating in an organised race, but jogging to keep fit or doing a fun run is physical recreation. Cycling is another example of a leisure activity that can be either an informal physical recreation or a serious sport.

Professional sports participants, such as footballers and athletes, contribute to the leisure of the people who watch them — spectators. Sports spectating usually takes place where the match or sporting event is held (at a venue such as a stadium or racecourse). People may also watch sport on television at home or elsewhere (e.g. a televised football match screened in a pub).

The **arts and entertainment** key component covers leisure activities that are creative or involve a performance — on stage or screen. Leisure activities in arts and entertainment are usually those of viewing works of art like paintings or watching a film or show. Professional artists and entertainers create and perform as their paid work. Their activity is not leisure for them, but it is part of the leisure industry because they are providing enjoyment for other people. Some people like to paint for pleasure or to act on the amateur stage for fun. For these people, art and performing are leisure activities.

Countryside recreation means leisure activities that take place in rural areas away from towns or cities. Angling, rambling, horse riding and mountain biking are common in countryside locations, including National Parks and Areas of Outstanding Natural Beauty. Of course, anglers can be seen on urban canals and river banks and people ride mountain bikes on city streets, but these leisure activities are typical of rural areas.

Home-based leisure covers any leisure activity that people engage in at home: they do not go out to do it. Some home-based leisure activities are passive, such as watching television, playing on a computer or reading a book. Other activities that are more physically active include gardening or DIY (do-it-yourself). These are done as a hobby rather than out of economic necessity. Some home-based leisure activities may involve bringing a product into the home (like a hired video) or having one delivered (such as a take-away meal) from a facility that provides products and services for the home leisure market (e.g. video-rental shops and take-away restaurants).

Children's play activities can be informal and take place in different settings. Traditional games include hide-and-seek, ball games and running around outdoors in playgrounds, parks, streets and on beaches. Electronic play using sophisticated technical devices is a feature of the modern world. Today's leisure industry makes provision for more formal, organised play through facilities such as playgrounds, ball parks and adventure playgrounds and also through programmes such as play schemes and 'art fun' courses at libraries and arts centres during the school holidays. Play is a children's

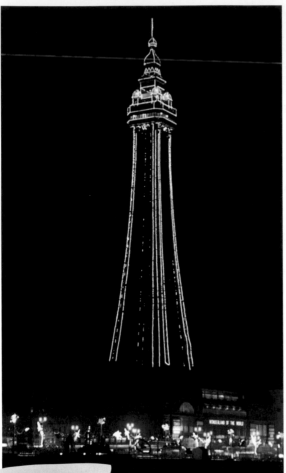

▲ *Figure 1.4*
Blackpool Tower
illuminated at night

leisure activity, but preschool classes are not — they amount to work for young children, just as formal education can be seen as the work of their older friends (and work is *not* leisure). Facilities such as crèches and services such as child-minding are not parts of the leisure industry when they provide childcare to enable an adult to go to work.

Visitor attractions seek to draw people to them for leisure. Some visitor attractions are historic sites, such as castles, stately homes, cathedrals and ancient monuments like Stonehenge and Hadrian's Wall. More modern visitor attractions include facilities such as theme parks and the fairgrounds and amusements found at places like seaside resorts. Blackpool Tower (Figure 1.4) is a famous seaside attraction on the Lancashire seaside resort's 'Golden Mile' of amusements and operates in conjunction with the Pleasure Beach theme park. The Blackpool Illuminations in autumn and the town's historic trams (which still run along the promenade) are visitor attractions in themselves. People who live in Blackpool can enjoy the resort's attractions, but visitors from elsewhere (tourists) are the main customers. Visiting attractions can be a leisure activity for both local people and tourists.

Catering is provided at many visitor attractions. This key component is concerned with serving food and drink products to customers. Everything from a can of fizzy drink or bottle of water from a vending machine to a full restaurant meal is a catering component product. It is the enjoyment of the products and service provided by catering facilities that is the leisure activity. Activities such as going out for a meal or enjoying an ice cream in a café or a drink in a bar belong to the catering component. Examples of types of facilities included in catering are shown in Figure 1.5, along with types of facility for other components. Figure 1.6 gives examples of leisure activities that belong to each of the leisure industry's key components.

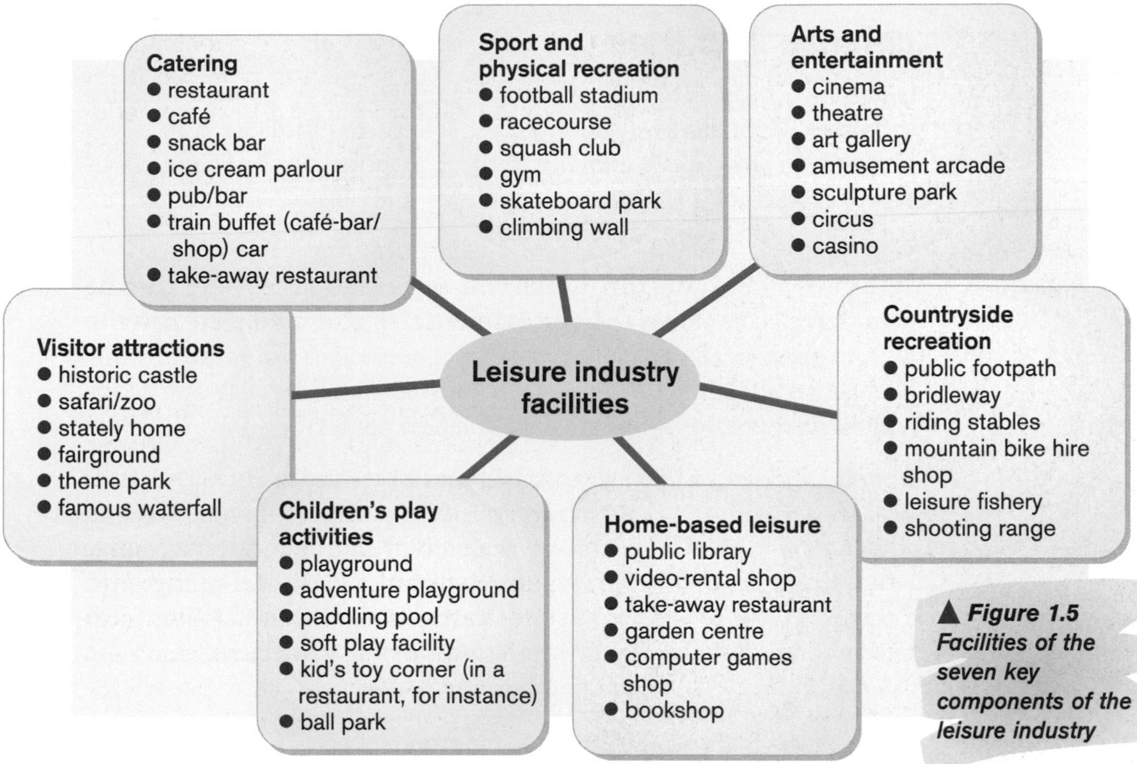

must to know

Catering
- restaurant
- café
- snack bar
- ice cream parlour
- pub/bar
- train buffet (café-bar/ shop) car
- take-away restaurant

Sport and physical recreation
- football stadium
- racecourse
- squash club
- gym
- skateboard park
- climbing wall

Arts and entertainment
- cinema
- theatre
- art gallery
- amusement arcade
- sculpture park
- circus
- casino

Visitor attractions
- historic castle
- safari/zoo
- stately home
- fairground
- theme park
- famous waterfall

Leisure industry facilities

Countryside recreation
- public footpath
- bridleway
- riding stables
- mountain bike hire shop
- leisure fishery
- shooting range

Children's play activities
- playground
- adventure playground
- paddling pool
- soft play facility
- kid's toy corner (in a restaurant, for instance)
- ball park

Home-based leisure
- public library
- video-rental shop
- take-away restaurant
- garden centre
- computer games shop
- bookshop

▲ *Figure 1.5*
Facilities of the seven key components of the leisure industry

Catering
- eating in a restaurant
- ordering a snack in a café
- having a drink in a pub
- buying 'street food' in a city
- being served refreshments on a train
- enjoying popcorn in a cinema

Sport and physical recreation
- playing netball
- cycling
- swimming
- ice skating
- running
- skateboarding

Arts and entertainment
- watching a film
- attending a play
- viewing art
- amateur acting
- karaoke
- listening to music

Visitor attractions
- touring a historic building
- riding a theme-park rollercoaster
- sightseeing in a city
- visiting a beauty spot
- photographing a famous waterfall
- interacting in a museum

Leisure industry activities

Countryside recreation
- angling
- bird watching
- shooting
- rambling
- horse riding
- mountain biking

Children's play activities
- playing in a playground
- having fun in a ball park
- board gaming
- splashing in a paddling pool
- building sandcastles
- making a snowman

Home-based leisure
- computer gaming
- watching a video
- gardening
- do-it-yourself (for fun)
- reading a book
- eating a take-away meal

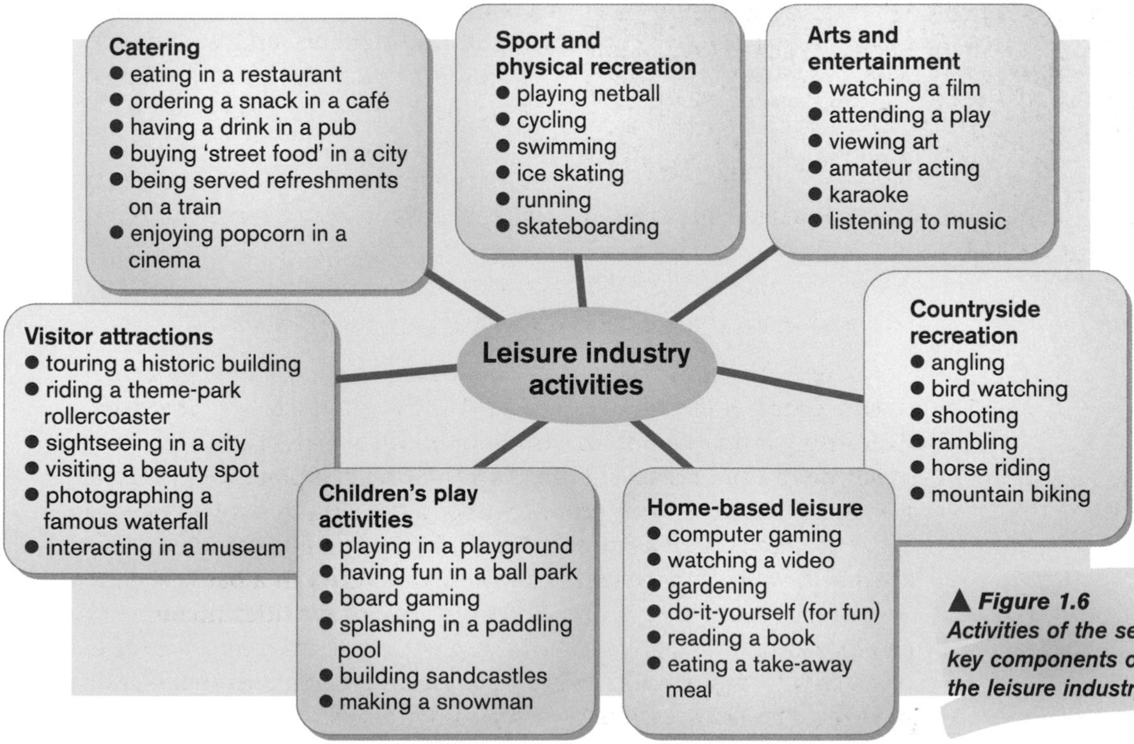

▲ *Figure 1.6*
Activities of the seven key components of the leisure industry

Leisure facilities

Leisure facilities are places where organisations provide leisure activities. These may be buildings, e.g. a leisure centre (see Figure 1.9) or outdoor sites, e.g. a playing field or a sports pitch. Examples of types of facility belonging to each of the leisure industry's key components are given in Figure 1.5.

Leisure facilities are run by leisure organisations. These can be commercial companies or non-commercial organisations, such as the Leisure Services Department of the local council or voluntary groups like sports clubs. (The differences between commercial and non-commercial organisations are explained on page 11.)

▼ *Figure 1.7
Leisure facilities in
Darlington town
centre*

In any area there will be a range of types of leisure facility. The practical scenario in this section is about investigating home-based leisure somewhere in the UK. Figure 1.7 is a plan of Darlington town centre, where examples of different types of facility are located. Darlington is a town in County Durham in the northeast of England. Towns local to you might have similar facilities to those described here.

	Key component	Name of facility	Type of facility
1	Sport and physical recreation	Dolphin Centre	Leisure centre
2	Arts and entertainment	Civic Theatre	Theatre
3	Home-based leisure	Blockbuster	Video-rental shop
4	Children's play activities	South Park	Children's play
5	Visitor attractions	Darlington Railway Museum	Museum
6	Catering	Imperial Express	Café

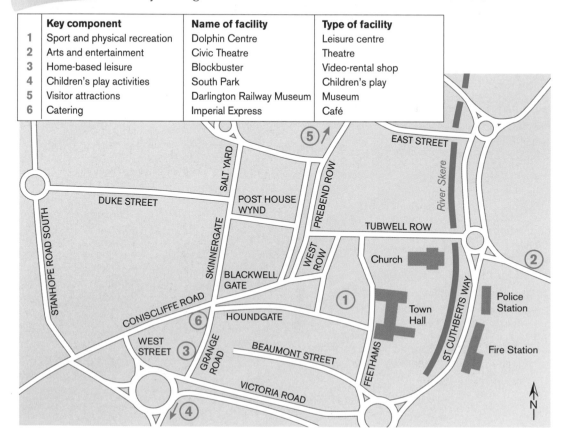

Crossing key components

Leisure activities and facilities can belong to more than one key component of the leisure industry. Horse riding is an activity that takes place usually in rural areas, away from towns and cities, so it belongs to the countryside recreation component. However, it is also form of a relaxation that involves using the body, so it is physical recreation. It can be done competitively, e.g. horse racing and show-jumping (Figure 1.8), so it can be a sport as well.

◀ *Figure 1.8 Showjumping: jumping across components*

▼ *Figure 1.9 A leisure centre: the Dolphin Centre in Darlington*

A **leisure centre** is a type of leisure facility that often crosses key components. Table 1.1 shows how this applies to the Dolphin Centre in Darlington (Figure 1.9).

Other facilities that operate in more than one key component of the leisure industry include:

- health clubs
- museums
- community centres
- sport venues

Stephen Rickerby

Key component	Inside the Dolphin Centre
Sport and physical recreation	Swimming pool
Children's play activities	'Topsy Turvy': cushioned, soft play environment
Catering	Restaurant

◀ *Table 1.1*

	Health club	Leisure centre
Example	Bannatyne's, Darlington	Dolphin Centre, Darlington
Customers	Club members	General public
Focus	Health and fitness	Broad range of leisure activities, including health and fitness
On offer	Swimming	Soft play
	Spabath, sauna and steam room	Crèche
	50 classes a week (e.g. pilates and yoga)	Swimming and swimming lessons
	3 aerobics studios	Water slides and children's pool
	Large gym with cardio theatre to watch television and listen to the radio during workouts	Diving pool
		Sports courses (e.g. football and athletics)
	Personal training	Conference facilities
	Massage	School-holiday play schemes
	Tanning	Fitness suites and exercise programmes
	Café/bar	Restaurant

▼ *Figure 1.10 Bannatyne's health club in Darlington*

▲ *Table 1.2 Differences between a health club and a leisure centre*

Stephen Rickerby

Some differences between **health clubs** and leisure centres are listed in Table 1.2. Figure 1.10 shows a Bannatyne's health club in Darlington.

Community centres offer a range of simpler facilities, including a function room and kitchen, for the public for hire. Customers can organise their own social events such as parties. There is often a programme of leisure activities organised in the form of classes (e.g. aerobics) or clubs (e.g. ballroom dancing). The purpose of community centres, which are not run commercially, is to provide for the social welfare of the local community. In some rural areas, the village hall does the same job. Figure 1.11 shows the village hall in Bishopton, a village near Darlington.

Stephen Rickerby

▲ *Figure 1.11 Bishopton village hall near Darlington*

Museums are visitor attractions that can offer catering facilities and host arts and entertainment events, such as exhibitions of paintings or sculptures and small-scale musical performances. Nationally important museums are described on pages 23–25.

Sports venues are the places where sporting events are held. A stadium is an example of a sports venue — Figure 1.12 shows the stadium used by Darlington FC soccer team. Of course, sports venues belong to the sports and physical recreation key component, but they usually cross into others. Catering is often provided by fast-food outlets, bars or restaurants. Stadia can be hired out to host other events such as pop and rock concerts, which brings them into the arts and entertainment key component. In some large cities (e.g. Manchester and Newcastle upon Tyne), there are large indoor arenas that are used both for arts and entertainment events and as sports venues.

◀ *Figure 1.12 Darlington FC stadium*

Stephen Rickerby

Commercial and non-commercial organisations

Commercial leisure organisations are privately owned by individuals or by companies. These organisations run leisure facilities to make a profit by selling leisure products and services to their customers. Facilities shown in Figure 1.7 that are run by commercial organisations are:

- the video-rental shop owned by Blockbuster (a company-run facility)
- the Imperial Express café (a privately owned business)

Non-commercial organisations are facilities run by government or councils or are voluntary groups like sports clubs. Examples of facilities run by non-commercial organisations in Darlington town centre (Figure 1.7) are the Dolphin Centre, the Civic Theatre, the children's playground and the railway museum. Darlington Borough Council is the main controlling interest and runs these facilities on behalf of the public.

Have a Go

Know and understand	Apply what you know	Investigate

Know and understand

1 a Collect pictures of leisure activities. Make a chart that organises them into key components.

b Design a Power-Point presentation to show what makes up any **one** key component of the leisure industry.

c Explain how leisure centres and health clubs differ.

Apply what you know

2 a Brainstorm a list of leisure facilities in your local town. Classify the facilities into key components.

b Collect leaflets and flyers that are used in marketing leisure facilities. (Flyers have only one page, but leaflets fold into several panels.)

Evaluate how well **one** of the flyers/leaflets promotes its facility.

c Design a flyer for a leisure facility. The flyer should be eye-catching and include:
- what is on offer
- where the facility is
- prices
- contact details

Investigate

3 a Research examples of leisure facilities provided in your local town centre.

b Produce an annotated map that locates the examples and gives brief details of leisure products and services they offer.

Products and services

Types of products and services

A leisure facility can often provide a range of products and services. Table 1.2 (page 10) lists what the Dolphin Centre (a leisure centre in Darlington) offers its customers. Items in the list are not necessarily products and services in themselves. For example, the swimming pool is a facility within a facility. The swimming-pool product that customers buy may be admission for a swimming session or a course of lessons. Services include the lifeguards present at the poolside and the teaching provided by the swimming instructors.

In the café bar at Bannatyne's health club, food and drink products are sold and are served to customers by the staff that work there. It is clear from Table 1.2 that both Bannatyne's and the Dolphin Centre provide leisure products and services that cross boundaries between the key components of the leisure industry.

Different needs

The leisure industry provides different products and services to try to meet the needs of a variety of customer types. Leisure is about how people use their spare time and people have different ideas about how to enjoy themselves at various times. While one person may enjoy a visit to an art gallery, another may prefer an evening out at a disco. However, the customer of the art gallery may enjoy the disco another time. Factors that help people to decide their choice of leisure activities are examined on pages 39–41.

Customers of leisure facilities can be classified according to:
- interests — what they enjoy
- age — children, teenagers, young adults, older people
- group size — individuals, couples, small groups, large parties
- income — restricted or large disposable incomes
- special needs — access, culture, language

What people enjoy doing can be related to their age group, but different people of similar age can like different leisure activities. Think of the members of your class. Although you are probably of similar age, and many of you will have similar interests, there will be differences. The same is true for older people. A pensioner may enjoy reading quietly or dancing. Leisure facilities need to cater for different sizes of group. A café will cope easily with people coming in unannounced on their own, with a partner or with a small group of friends. However, the owners may find that they need to organise a reservation system in order to provide good customer service for larger parties.

People have different amounts of money to spend on leisure activities. Usually this depends on how much money they earn — their income. People pursue leisure activities in the time left over after work, sleep and taking care of life's essentials (such as shopping for food). The money that they spend on leisure is what is left after paying for basic needs such as housing, food and heating, as well as saving for the future. People's leisure spending comes out of their disposable income, which is the money they have left after covering all their necessities. Levels of disposable income vary from person to person and between age groups.

Every customer of a leisure facility can have particular requirements, and so everyone has their own special needs. However, in planning the products and services that they offer to their customers, the managers of leisure facilities take several practical factors into account. One of these is access. This means how easy it is for all customers to enter and use the leisure facility. Access issues can arise for people whose mobility is limited — if they use a wheelchair, for example. Similarly, special consideration may need to be given to customers with impaired hearing or eyesight, or who do not

Activity	Meeting different needs	Factors considered
Waterslides	Fun for children above 8 years old	Age
Swimming lessons	From parent-and-toddler classes to water-polo lessons for teenagers	Age and interest
Fun with inflatables	Saturday afternoon disco float session with guest DJ	Age
Birthday parties (for ages 8+ only)	Pool party, no slides £46 Pool party, with slides £67	Income level and age
Swimming-pool use with a small child	Prams and pushchairs cannot be taken onto poolside An area is provided where they can be locked away	Special needs
Family restaurant meal	Children's meals are available, as are high chairs and a play area for preschool children	Age, group size (family) and special needs

▲ **Table 1.3 Swim-related children's activities at the Dolphin Centre**

understand English or Welsh, so that they have maximum access to what the facility has to offer. Wheelchair ramps, hearing loops, textured walking routes and signs in languages other than English or Welsh are among widespread solutions to access issues in leisure facilities.

Table 1.3 shows some of the children's swimming activities on offer at the Dolphin Centre in Darlington and how these are meant to meet different people's needs. Of course, many Dolphin Centre customers are not engaged in swim-related activities or are not there with children, so the management of the Dolphin Centre must try to satisfy the needs of a wide variety of customers. This is true of leisure facilities throughout the UK.

Changes over the last 20 years

The leisure industry has developed over many years. As people's leisure needs have changed, the industry has adapted to provide for those needs. Over the last 20 years, each of the key components of the industry has been affected:

- **Sport and physical recreation**: one example has been the growth of health clubs. Often located on leisure parks or on inner-city re-development sites, health clubs like Bannatyne's in Darlington have satisfied increased demand for indoor gym and other fitness facilities.
- **Arts and entertainment**: more cinemas have moved out of town. More multiplex cinemas (Figure 1.3) have been developed on the edges of towns and cities. They are often located on leisure parks. It is easier to drive to cinemas out of town than to town-centre cinemas. In addition, multiplex cinemas can offer a wider choice of films on show at any one time.

- **Countryside recreation**: there are now more designated country parks, picnic areas and specified walkways. Increased health consciousness and awareness of the rural environment has led more people to want to access the countryside easily. Local councils have responded by marking public rights of way and providing increased information and services such as guided walks at weekends.

- **Home-based leisure**: technology has changed substantially and there are more computers and sophisticated electronic gaming devices. The introduction of DVDs to the film-rental market has affected video-rental shops. There has been a move away from small, often independently owned facilities, which have been replaced by larger premises owned by national chains. A chain is a series of similar facilities run by the same organisation with branches in different places. Modern film-rental shops offer a variety of services such as 24-hour drop-offs for returning DVDs and products including snacks and confectionery to take home with the rented film.

- **Children's play activities**: play barns have been developed along with more family pubs. Leisure organisations that own pubs have done this to encourage more families to eat and drink in their facilities. Elsewhere in the leisure industry, the provision of children's play alongside the main product has also been increasing.

- **Visitor attractions**: new technology has made museums more interactive with exhibits that younger visitors in particular can enjoy more. Attractions such as Eureka! in Halifax, West Yorkshire and the Life Centre in Newcastle upon Tyne are examples of facilities that have been part of this trend. Theme parks have needed to compete with each other and with attractions overseas like Disneyland Paris. They have developed more sophisticated, more daring 'white-knuckle' rides to persuade more customers to visit them.

- **Catering**: family restaurant chains have spread more widely, particularly on leisure parks near other facilities such as multiplex cinemas and bowling alleys. Leisure parks themselves have developed considerably to provide leisure experiences for customers using more than one facility in a single visit. For example, a birthday party for a 10-year-old may include bowling followed by a meal at a family restaurant on the site. Fast-food outlets, including those on leisure parks, have increasingly become drive-through facilities.

√ Leisure in different places

The range of leisure facilities provided in one place in the UK can be different from those that exist in another place. Although the facilities offered in leisure parks may be similar, there can be significant differences between what is provided in different parts of a town. Town centres have a wider range of facilities than suburban housing estates, and the facilities in rural localities often differ from those in a city.

Figure 1.13 summarises the types of leisure facility found in different places.

▶ *Figure 1.13*
Leisure in different locations

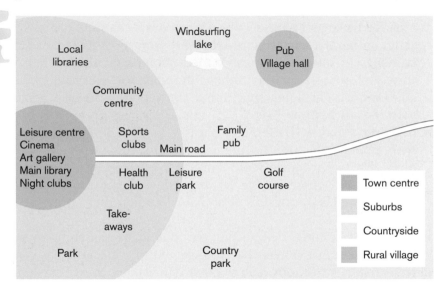

Have a Go

Know and understand

1 Explain how the Dolphin Centre in Darlington has adapted its children's activities to meet the needs of different customers.

Apply what you know

2 For a leisure facility you know about, describe how it meets the needs of **three** different types of customer.

Investigate

3 a Interview an older person about changes in leisure provision in your local area in the last 20 years.

b Compare the leisure provision in **one** key component in **two** different places chosen from:
- a town centre
- a leisure park
- a suburban housing estate
- a rural village

Investigating leisure

Local leisure facilities in and around a town in the UK are likely to include:

- leisure centres and health clubs
- swimming pools and sports grounds
- parks and gardens
- libraries
- country parks and picnic sites
- museums and galleries
- theatres and cinemas
- restaurants, nightclubs and public houses

Other examples are take-away restaurants and facilities that provide for home-based leisure. The functions and the location of home-based leisure facilities are described and explained on pages 38–39.

Practical scenario Investigating leisure provision in an area

The flowchart in Figure 1.14 shows steps that can be taken to investigate the leisure industry in an area such as a local town centre. It may be more efficient to carry out such an investigation as a team, sharing the work out between different team members.

▼ *Figure 1.14 Flowchart for investigating leisure in a local area*

Outcomes

The results of such an investigation can be presented in:

- a booklet about leisure in the town centre
- a wall chart
- a PowerPoint presentation
- a written or word-processed report
- a video

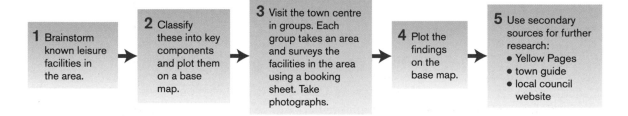

1 Brainstorm known leisure facilities in the area.

2 Classify these into key components and plot them on a base map.

3 Visit the town centre in groups. Each group takes an area and surveys the facilities in the area using a booking sheet. Take photographs.

4 Plot the findings on the base map.

5 Use secondary sources for further research:
- Yellow Pages
- town guide
- local council website

Chapter 1.2

√ National leisure facilities

Leisure facilities in local areas are provided mainly for residents. They include leisure centres and health clubs, cinemas and theatres, picnic sites and country parks, video-rental shops and libraries, museums and historic buildings, restaurants and pubs. Visitors to the local area may make use of these local facilities as well, especially those that are visitor attractions or that belong to the catering key component.

Leisure facilities can also be important nationally and address the needs of people from all over the UK and sometimes beyond. Different categories of national leisure facilities are:

- recreation centres of excellence
- sports venues
- museums and galleries
- tourist attractions
- theme parks
- historic sites

In this chapter we look at recreation centres of excellence, sports venues, museums and galleries. Chapter 1.3 covers tourist attractions, theme parks and historic sites.

Recreation centres of excellence

Bisham Abbey, Crystal Palace, Holme Pierrepoint and Lilleshall are recreation centres of excellence in England. Each centre provides elite athletes with a range of specialist facilities, equipment, expertise and residential accommodation suitable for training and competition. The better the athletes perform, the greater the country's success in international competitions like the Olympic Games. These centres of excellence offer facilities for the general public too, including conference facilities, as well as beginners' and improvers' courses in most of the leisure activities that take place at each site.

Glenmore Lodge in Scotland and Plas-y-Brenin in north Wales are both mountain centres, specialising in mountain sports and outdoor activities.

Table 1.4 summarises the purposes of six nationally important recreation centres that are located on the map in Figure 1.15.

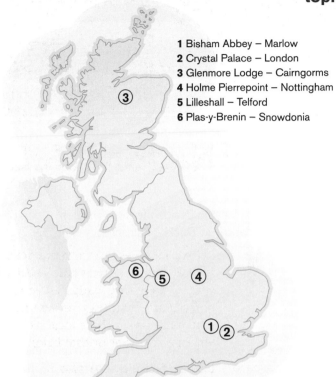

1 Bisham Abbey – Marlow
2 Crystal Palace – London
3 Glenmore Lodge – Cairngorms
4 Holme Pierrepoint – Nottingham
5 Lilleshall – Telford
6 Plas-y-Brenin – Snowdonia

▶ *Figure 1.15*
Six national recreation centres of excellence

▼ *Table 1.4 Purpose and locations of national recreation centres*

National recreation centre	Main purpose	Location
Bisham Abbey	Training for top-class sports participants Includes a £1.2 million international hockey pitch and a judo hall for the National British Judo Academy	Beside the River Thames near Marlow in Buckinghamshire
Crystal Palace	National centre for training International athletics stadium Indoor facilities including four swimming pools	South London
Glenmore Lodge	National Outdoor Training Centre for Scotland. Centre for teaching participants and training instructors in: • mountain sports (climbing and mountain biking) • paddle sports (kayaking) • first aid and rescue	Cairngorm National Park in Scotland
Holme Pierrepoint	Focuses on water sports with: • regatta lake with an international standard 2,000 m six-lane rowing course • white-water canoe slalom course • water-ski lagoon with slalom course	Beside River Trent, near Nottingham
Lilleshall	National sports teams training centre British Olympic Association accreditation for gymnastics and archery Other sports include tennis, cricket, squash and bowls	Near Telford in Shropshire
Plas-y-Brenin	National Mountain Centre offering courses including: skiing, kayaking, climbing, mountain adventure, Duke of Edinburgh awards	Snowdonia National Park in north Wales

CaseStudy   Bisham Abbey

Set in the grounds of a twelfth-century abbey, Bisham Abbey was the first official National Sports Centre. Sporting activities started at Bisham Abbey in 1947, but the first proper sports centre there opened only in 1974.

Location

Bisham Abbey is located beside the River Thames, 1.5 km from Marlow in Buckinghamshire, south-east England.

Purpose

Each sport in the UK is controlled by an organisation called a governing body. For soccer this is the Football Association. Several governing bodies use the Bisham Abbey national recreation centre as a base and to train elite competitors, including:

- British Judo Association
- Football Association
- British Weightlifting Association
- Rugby Football Union

Bisham Abbey is the base for the National Judo Academy (Figure 1.16), which prepares Britain's best judo participants for major championships such as the Olympic Games. This sports centre also provides training opportunities for top athletes who take part in other sports including hockey and women's rowing. The facilities at Bisham Abbey are open to the general public as well. Grass pitches and tennis courts are available, as well as a nine-hole golf course and an astroturf hockey pitch.

The sports centre has recently undergone re-development costing £11 million. The new building has:

- a new fitness centre
- squash courts
- indoor tennis courts
- a weightlifting area
- two dojos for judo training
- a café/bar
- offices for the resident governing bodies
- a revamped sports injuries clinic and sports-science area

Bisham Abbey is also a conference centre and can be booked by businesses and members of the public for private functions such as Christmas parties and wedding receptions.

▲ *Figure 1.16 National Judo Academy, Bisham Abbey*

Sports venues

Sports venues are where competitions such as races and matches take place. Nationally important sports venues include the stadia of the principal teams that play in the football premiership and those venues listed in Table 1.5. Figure 1.17 shows the locations of these venues.

Sport	Venue	Location	Main purpose
Soccer	Hampden Park	Glasgow	Home ground for Scotland's national team
	Windsor Park	Belfast	Home ground for Northern Ireland's national team
Rugby	Landsdowne Road	Dublin	Ireland rugby union teams' home ground
	Millennium Stadium	Cardiff	Home ground for Wales
	Murrayfield	Edinburgh	Home ground for Scotland
	Twickenham	South London	England's home stadium
Cricket	Lord's	North London	Headquarters for the sport and principal national cricket venue
Hockey	National Hockey Stadium	Milton Keynes, Buckinghamshire	Headquarters of the English Hockey Association
Tennis	Wimbledon	South London	Headquarters of the All England Lawn Tennis Club and setting for its annual championships, often regarded as the most important in the world

▲ **Table 1.5**
Important national sports venues

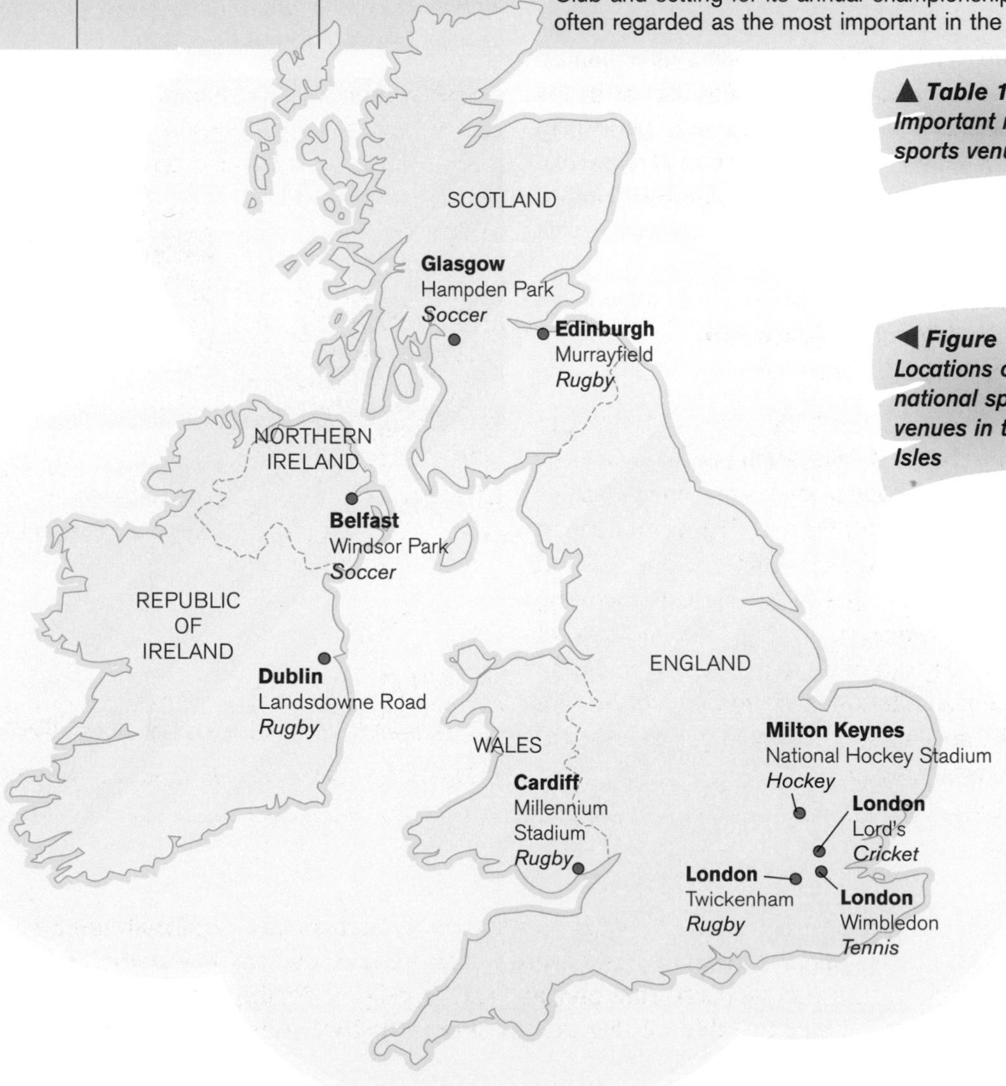

◄ **Figure 1.17**
Locations of some national sports venues in the British Isles

CaseStudy Millennium Stadium, Cardiff

Location

The **Millennium Stadium** (Figure 1.18) is in central Cardiff, between the Central (railway) Station and Cardiff Castle. Cardiff is the capital city of Wales, located in the south of the country. Figure 1.19 gives more detail and shows typical car journey times to the Millennium Stadium.

Purpose

Cardiff's Millennium Stadium is the base for Welsh Rugby Union and is where the Welsh team plays its home matches. It is also used for other important rugby matches, such as the 2006 final of the Heineken Cup. The Welsh soccer team plays there too and, during the reconstruction of London's Wembley Stadium, important English football matches have been staged there, as have events for other sports such as motorcycling.

Like many sports venues, the Millennium Stadium has secondary purposes:

- concerts and music festivals, including rock and pop bands
- party venue (e.g. 'The Night it Snowed in Vegas' Christmas series in 2005)
- conference centre, hosting business conferences, meetings and dinners in seven suites of rooms

It also offers hospitality facilities to businesses, such as the hire of executive boxes in which managers can entertain corporate clients and enjoy an excellent view of the day's match.

Figure 1.18 The Millennium Stadium in Cardiff

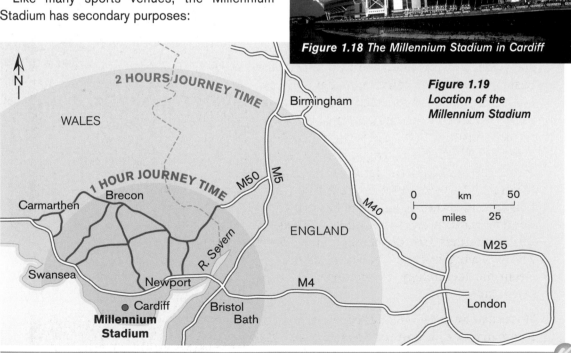

Figure 1.19
Location of the
Millennium Stadium

Have a Go

Know and understand	Apply what you know	Investigate
1 a Compare a local leisure centre with a national recreation centre. **b** Explain why national recreation centres and sports venues often act as conference centres.	**2 a** The Millennium Stadium is a London Olympics 2012 venue. Use Figure 1.19 to help you to describe the route from London to Cardiff. **b i** List **three** principal teams that are currently members of the football premiership. **ii** Describe the location and purpose of one principal soccer premiership stadium.	**3 a** Research forthcoming events at the Millennium Stadium in Cardiff. **b** Present a case-study report on a national recreation centre other than Bisham Abbey.

Museums and galleries

Museums

Museums look after objects and documents from the past. These are cared for, or conserved, so that people can learn about life in the past and appreciate the achievements of previous generations. Museum collections are managed by curators, who look after items for the benefit of future generations.

Museums belong to the visitor attractions key component of the leisure industry. They are leisure facilities because members of the public come to view collections in their spare time and out of interest. Some museums attract visitors by organising special exhibitions based round a particular theme that run for limited lengths of time (Figure 1.20). This is part of marketing the museum. In recent years, there has been a trend for more interactive exhibits. Visitors can sometimes handle objects, chat to actors playing historic characters or use electronic technology to enhance their experience.

Museums are often controlled by non-commercial organisations. Some charge for admission, but others are free to

▼ *Figure 1.20*
A promotional leaflet for an exhibition at the British Museum in London

THE BRITISH MUSEUM

What's on

Celebrating Chinese New Year with activities and performance for all ages – see page 8

enter. National museums are run for the benefit of the entire nation and receive money from the UK government so that they do not need to charge for admission. Nevertheless, running a museum and caring for its precious objects is expensive, so customers may be invited to make a donation and are charged for additional products and services such as cloakrooms, guidebooks and audio-tours. An audio-tour involves an electronic playback device, with headphones, that customers can listen to as they explore the museum. Museums, including the free-entry national museums, sometimes charge for admission to specially staged exhibitions.

Art galleries

Art galleries function as leisure facilities in a similar way to museums. They attract visitors to view the works of art for which they care and which they exhibit. Most art galleries have a 'standing collection': paintings, sculptures and other works of art that the gallery owns or that have been lent to it on a permanent basis. Depending on space, only part of this standing collection is on display at any one time. The rest is kept in storage or lent to other galleries for temporary exhibitions.

In addition to the standing collection, art galleries can mount one-off exhibitions based around a theme or the work of a famous artist. They may borrow works of art to include in the exhibition or simply put some of their standing collection together in a different way.

▼ *Table 1.6 Some nationally important museums and art galleries*

Some nationally important museums and art galleries are listed in Table 1.6 and Figure 1.21.

Facility	Name	Location	Theme
Museums	Beamish Museum	County Durham, northeast England	Open-air museum of life in the industrial north of England
	British Museum	Central London	Civilisations from around the world
	Ironbridge Gorge	Near Telford in Shropshire	Industrial Revolution
	Natural History Museum	Kensington, London	Plant and animal life
	National Museum of Photography, Film and Television	Bradford	Still and moving images
	National Railway Museum	York	Railway heritage
	Royal Armouries	Leeds	Armaments in war and peace
	Science Museum	Kensington, London	Technology and science
Art galleries	The National Gallery	Trafalgar Square, London	European paintings
	Tate Britain	Central London	British art
	Tate Modern	South Bank, London	Modern art

Purposes

The main leisure industry purpose of the museums and galleries listed in Table 1.6 is to attract visitors to view their collections. The principal theme of each collection is listed in the table. Museums and galleries want people to enjoy their visits and see themselves as having a mission to educate. They offer tours for student groups and employ education officers to arrange learning programmes for school and college students.

Another purpose of these facilities is conservation. Collections are carefully looked after and restored for the benefit of future generations. Museums and galleries need to make money so that their collections can be protected and made available for the public to see. Catering services and gift shops are important sources of income for museums and galleries.

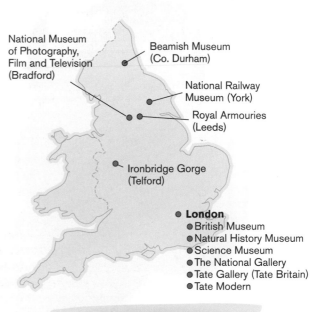

▲ *Figure 1.21 Locations of nationally important museums and art galleries*

CaseStudy   Tate Modern

Tate Modern (Figure 1.22) is one of four Tate galleries in the UK. Tate Britain — the original Tate Gallery — is another. Tate Modern was founded in 2000.

Location

Tate Modern is on the southern bank of the River Thames in central London. It is in a building that used to be Bankside power station. The Millennium footbridge connects it to the City of London on the opposite bank.

Along the River Thames to the west of Tate Modern is the South Bank — an area in which there are a number of leisure industry facilities, many of which are also tourist attractions (Figure 1.23). Close to the London Eye and Westminster Bridge is the National Theatre.

Figure 1.22 Tate Modern

© Angelo Hornak/CORBIS

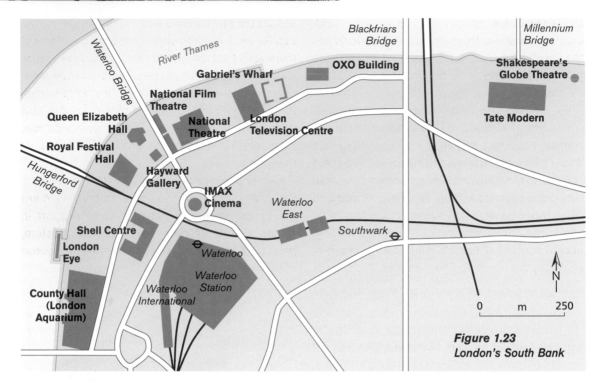

Figure 1.23
London's South Bank

Purpose

The main function of Tate Modern is to exhibit new and modern works of art from the UK and abroad. Sometimes this art is controversial, as shown by the news report in Figure 1.24. Tate Modern defines modern art as works created since 1900. Its standing collection includes the work of famous artists such as Pablo Picasso and Andy Warhol. This collection is displayed in four themed areas of the gallery. Each area is based on a subject that

Turner shortlist show unveiled

Tomoko Takahashi's work fills an entire gallery with junk

A room full of junk designed to suggest the aftermath of an earthquake has been unveiled as the Turner Prize shortlist exhibition opens.

The work, Learning How To Drive by Japanese artist Tomoko Takahashi, features twisted steering wheels, bollards, traffic signs, discarded hubcaps and tyres.

Controversy

The annual prize which seeks to reward challenging modern art has been condemned in recent years by critics as 'an ongoing national joke'.

Tate spokesman Simon Wilson said: 'The prize always generates controversy but it does bring together young artists who are doing fresh innovative work.'

Source: BBC

▲ *Figure 1.24 News extract about controversy at Tate Modern*

artists use a lot: history, the human form, land-scape and still life. This means that leisure visitors can decide to explore just one area in a visit to the gallery. Audio-tours (including a children's version) are available.

As well as exhibiting its standing collection, Tate Modern has a continuous series of temporary exhibitions. Leisure customers may return to Tate Modern in later visits because they are attracted by temporary exhibitions. The programme of these exhibitions is updated often and can be found on the gallery's website (**www.tate.org.uk/modern**).

Like many museums and galleries, Tate Modern has the purpose of helping customers to interpret what they see, using written notices, audio-tours and an online multimedia tour. The Clore Information Room is open to visitors who want to find out more about the art and artists. The gallery organises talks, lectures, gallery tours, discussions, courses and workshops. There are programmes to help school and college students, families and community groups to find out more. In addition, there are film screenings and performances of music and drama.

Catering provision at Tate Modern includes a restaurant, a café and an espresso bar, which are run by the gallery to raise funds to support it. Shops at Tate Modern sell art books, posters, postcards and souvenirs — another useful source of income.

Have a Go

Know and understand

1 Use Figure 1.21 and Table 1.6 to help you to make a wall chart about major museums and galleries in the UK.

Apply what you know

2 Use Figure 1.23 to describe the range of leisure and tourism attractions on London's South Bank.

Investigate

3 a i Research a list of forthcoming exhibitions or events at Tate Modern.

ii Recommend the one most likely to appeal to a family with school-age children.

b Make a PowerPoint presentation about the location and purpose of one of the museums shown in Table 1.6.

Chapter

1.3

Visitor attractions

Major museums and galleries are national leisure facilities. They are also visitor attractions. Other nationally important visitor attractions include theme parks and historic sites:

- Blackpool Tower and Pleasure Beach
- Bristol Zoo
- Chester Zoo
- Jorvik Viking Centre, York
- London Zoo
- Longleat Safari Park, Wiltshire
- Madame Tussaud's, London
- NEC (National Exhibition Centre), Birmingham
- Palace Pier, Brighton
- London Eye
- Woburn Safari Park, Bedfordshire

These visitor attractions are leisure facilities because customers go to them in their spare time for recreation. They are well known and attract visitors from outside the local area. Visitors who travel away from the place where they live and work are tourists. So the visitor attractions listed above are tourist attractions, too, as are the museums and galleries named in Chapter 1.2 and the theme parks and historic sites described later in this chapter. Attractions that are both leisure and tourism facilities demonstrate the links between leisure and tourism, which are discussed in Chapter 1.7.

Zoos and safari parks

Figure 1.25 shows the locations of the UK's major zoos and safari parks. London Zoo is in Regent's Park in central London. Chester Zoo and Bristol Zoo Gardens (in Clifton) are on the outskirts of their respective cities. The word 'zoo' is a shortened version of 'zoological gardens'. Zoos keep animals in captivity in enclosures and buildings set in landscaped grounds. As leisure facilities they attract visitors to see the animals for enjoyment and out of interest. Other purposes of zoos include animal research, protecting endangered species and education. They are similar to museums and galleries in selling the experience of viewing and learning from a collection and in having catering and book or gift shopping on site. It is the nature of their collections and the fact that they are typically outdoor attractions (with some indoor areas) that make zoos different.

Zoos were popular in Victorian times (the nineteenth century), when collectors brought exotic species back from expeditions around the world. In a time before film and television, zoos allowed their customers to view creatures that they could not otherwise see. In the twentieth century, there was concern about the animal-welfare issues linked with keeping animals in restricted cages and enclosures. Films, television wildlife programmes and increased car ownership have also helped to make safari parks popular attractions.

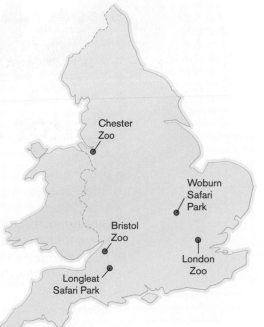

▲ **Figure 1.25**
Some major zoos and safari parks in the UK

In safari parks animals wander freely within a large area of grass, water and open woodland. Customers drive through the park and view the animals from their vehicles (Figure 1.26). Woburn and Longleat safari parks are located in the grounds of stately homes — country mansions owned by aristocratic families and opened to the public as leisure attractions.

◀ **Figure 1.26**
In a safari park

Adrian Sherratt/Alamy

Seaside attractions

Seaside towns and cities are covered in Chapter 1.6. Visitor attractions in two of the most popular seaside resorts are:

- Blackpool Tower and Pleasure Beach
- Palace Pier, Brighton

Blackpool Tower and Pleasure Beach are twinned attractions on the seafront. Blackpool Tower (Figure 1.4, page 6) is about 160 m tall and was completed in 1894. It is an indoor entertainment centre and has a playground, aquarium and historic ballroom with a world-famous Wurlitzer organ. The nearby Pleasure Beach is a large fairground with five roller coasters including the Pepsi Max Big One, and a themed children's area, Beaver Creek.

Palace Pier is in Brighton on the south coast of England. It dates from 1891 and supports a fairground, amusements, a restaurant, take-away food outlets and bars. Weddings and conferences are also arranged there.

Other major visitor attractions

Jorvik Viking Centre in York takes its name from the Viking name for the city. It features a reconstruction of the Viking streets that stood on the site 1,000 years ago with realistic sounds and smells. Employees play the roles of people of the time and answer questions posed by visitors. As well as being a straightforward leisure attraction, Jorvik is educational and is involved in archaeological preservation.

▼ *Figure 1.27
Inside a capsule on
the London Eye*

Madame Tussaud's near Baker Street underground station in London is next to another London visitor attraction: the London Planetarium. Wax figures of famous people past and present are exhibited. Interactivity has been a development of recent years, designed to enliven visits. Parties can be arranged there as well.

The London Eye is a giant Ferris wheel operated by British Airways. Passengers ride each 'flight' in transparent capsules (Figure 1.27) that afford views over London landmarks including Big Ben, Westminster Abbey and Buckingham Palace. The London Eye stands in central London, on the South Bank of the Thames, opposite and slightly downstream of the Houses of Parliament.

TopFoto

The NEC (National Exhibition Centre) on the eastern outskirts of Birmingham includes the 12,500-seat NEC Arena, which hosts shows and concerts (pop and classical) and sporting events like gymnastic championships and the Horse of the Year show. It is served by the M42 motorway and, for rail services, by Birmingham International station.

CaseStudy Bristol Zoo

Location

Bristol Zoo is in Clifton, 2 km from Bristol city centre in southwest England (see Figure 1.25). The M5 is the nearest motorway and car drivers are advised to exit at junction 17 and to take the A4018, following the brown and white elephant signs. Brown road signs are used in the UK to direct motorists to leisure and tourism facilities. The elephant symbol tells you that the attraction is a zoo and it does not need to be named on every sign. Figure 1.28 shows a brown tourist information road sign.

▲ *Figure 1.28 A tourist information road sign*

Purpose

Figure 1.29 is a plan of Bristol Zoo showing many of its leisure attractions. As well as exhibiting animals, Bristol Zoo provides catering services (the Pelican Restaurant is marked on the plan) and children's play activities (the Adventure Playground). It has educational and corporate hospitality purposes too. The Clifton Pavilion in the zoo grounds offers conference facilities, hosts weddings and is a venue for Christmas parties.

As a leisure facility, Bristol Zoo has diversified in other ways too. Events organised through the year include summer-evening theatrical performances and mother-and-toddler coffee mornings. These bring in more money directly and also market the zoo, because someone who comes to an event may be tempted to return as a paying customer of the zoo itself.

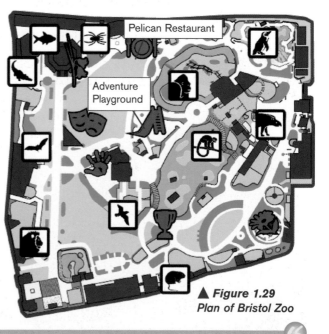

▲ *Figure 1.29*
Plan of Bristol Zoo

Theme parks

Theme parks are large, open areas with amusements, typically including 'white-knuckle' rides on exciting roller-coaster constructions. Customers may grip the handrails tightly (with white knuckles) as they spin round or soar up and down on the ride. Theme parks generally charge admission at the gate, selling day passes for example. Once inside the park, customers are free to choose which rides to go on and to return to their favourites as often as they like. However, at busy times the most popular rides can develop long queues. Some theme parks operate a 'fast pass' system in which customers can collect tickets to use the ride at a certain time. This reduces queuing time.

Major theme parks in the UK include:

- Alton Towers
- Chessington World of Adventures
- Thorpe Park
- Camelot
- LEGOLAND®

The locations of these theme parks are shown on Figure 1.30, which also includes major motorways.

▼ Figure 1.30 Major UK theme parks

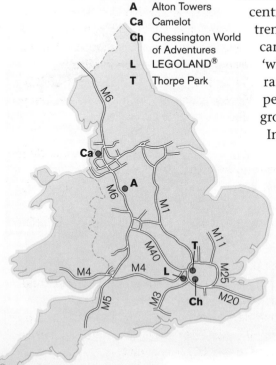

A   Alton Towers
Ca Camelot
Ch Chessington World of Adventures
L   LEGOLAND®
T   Thorpe Park

Theme parks were originally designed around a central theme. Disneyland in California began this trend with the theme of Walt Disney films and cartoon characters. Parks like Disneyland offer 'white-knuckle' rides but also provide a wider range of products and services, such as live performances, gentler and child-friendly fairground amusements and characters in costume. In the UK, Camelot in northwest England is based around the theme of King Arthur's court. LEGOLAND® in Windsor (southeast England) uses the LEGO construction toy as its base idea.

Other UK theme parks like Alton Towers attract visitors mainly because of the 'white-knuckle' entertainment that they offer. These rides have become the theme of the parks. Chessington World of Adventures in Surrey has grown from Chessington Zoo. It markets itself now as a family-friendly theme park with rides and other attractions aimed at families with younger children.

CaseStudy LEGOLAND® Windsor

Figure 1.31 is the front cover of a leaflet used to promote the LEGOLAND® Windsor theme park. Figure 1.32 shows the theme park's location.

▲ **Figure 1.31 LEGOLAND promotional leaflet (front cover)**

▲ **Figure 1.32 Location of LEGOLAND**

Location

LEGOLAND Windsor is 3 km west of Windsor town centre, close to junction 6 on the M4, which leads west from London's M25 orbital motorway. Although it is closer to the M4, LEGOLAND Windsor can also be reached from junction 3 on the M3.

Purpose

Originally based around the theme of the LEGO® construction toy, the park provides an enjoyable day out for families. Guests pay for admission and also spend money at the restaurants and cafés. Its other purposes are to make money and help to sell LEGO toys, as well as showcasing new LEGO product ranges and maintaining the park's position as one of the UK's leading tourist attractions. A family (its target market) features prominently on the promotional leaflet (Figure 1.31). Many of the rides and other attractions shown are themed around the LEGO bricks idea. A large LEGO model of London's Big Ben is featured in Miniland — a reconstruction, using plastic LEGO bricks, of world-famous buildings and landmarks. There is also a model of the London Eye.

Attractions and activities that serve LEGOLAND Windsor's main purpose of providing family fun include:

● Miniland
● rides (e.g. the Dragon Ride and Jungle Coaster)
● panning for gold in the Wild Woods
● live action shows, puppet shows and a 4-D movie
● driving small electric cars at the two LEGOLAND Driving Schools

Supporting the main purpose are:

● shops selling souvenirs, LEGO toys and themed children's clothes
● restaurants and cafés providing snacks (e.g. the Pit Stop Café's mini-doughnuts) and family meals at the 'Big Restaurant'
● birthday parties arranged by LEGOLAND Windsor's Corporate Events team

- annual passes that offer value for money and unlimited access for guests to return throughout the year; each annual pass is cheaper than visiting twice, so guests save money each time they enjoy the park

- short breaks including accommodation in nearby hotels
- group visits and company fun days for business tourists

Historic sites

Major historic sites in the UK (Figure 1.33) include:

- Beaulieu
- Buckingham Palace
- Chatsworth
- Hadrian's Wall
- Hampton Court Palace
- Stonehenge
- Tower of London

▶ **Figure 1.33**
Major UK historic sites

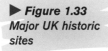

Hadrian's Wall

Chatsworth

Tower of London

Buckingham Palace

Stonehenge

Hampton Court Palace

Beaulieu

Publishing Pictures

Stonehenge and Hadrian's Wall

Stonehenge and Hadrian's Wall are ancient monuments. **Stonehenge** stands on Salisbury Plain and is a famous prehistoric site. It is a stone circle made up of sets of large stones assembled into arches by Stone Age people. The stones have survived for thousands of years and have long been a visitor attraction. The site, which is next to the A303 on Salisbury Plain, attracts particularly large numbers of visitors in June, on Midsummer's Day (the summer solstice), when the sun rises exactly over the Heel Stone just outside the main circle. The ancient builders of Stonehenge may have designed the circle with this phenomenon in mind.

Access to the stones themselves has been restricted because of the large numbers of people who want to visit them. Limited access lessens any negative impacts of tourism on Stonehenge and helps to conserve the monument for the future. This is called sustainable management. Impacts of tourism and sustainable tourism development are examined in detail in Chapter 1.6.

Hadrian's Wall was built around 2,000 years ago on the orders of the Roman Emperor Hadrian. It was to act as the border of the Roman Empire in Britain, and at that time ran from Wallsend near Newcastle upon Tyne to the Solway Firth on the west coast. Parts of what is sometimes simply called the Roman Wall have been partially reconstructed or excavated by archaeologists to become a series of leisure attractions. These include some stretches of the wall itself, such as the section near Housesteads in Northumberland which forms part of the Northumberland National Park (see Figure 1.34). Walking beside the wall is a cost-free physical and countryside recreation activity.

In addition, the remains of Roman forts such as Housesteads and Segundum at Wallsend have been developed into visitor attractions. At Vindolanda, just south of Housesteads, a museum and visitor

▼ **Figure 1.34**
Map of part of Hadrian's Wall

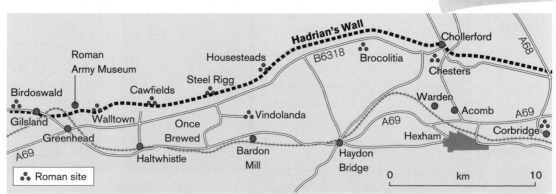

centre features reconstructions of Roman life. Like many leisure attractions, these have educational purposes as well as appealing to purely leisure visitors.

▼ *Figure 1.35 Yeomen of the Guard at the Tower of London*

Clay Perry/CORBIS

Hampton Court and the Tower of London

Hampton Court, which is beside the Thames to the southwest of London, and the Tower of London, close to Tower Bridge in central London, are both former royal palaces. **Hampton Court** was built for Cardinal Wolsey during the reign of Henry VIII and was later taken over by the king himself. Apart from the palace itself, one of its best-known attractions is the maze in its grounds.

The **Tower of London** has a long history as a castle, palace, prison and place of execution dating back to Norman times. Among those imprisoned and executed there was Henry VIII's second wife, Anne Boleyn. The Tower of London is home to the Crown Jewels, which many visitors see as part of their tour. Guided tours led by Yeomen of the Guard, also called Beefeaters, (see Figure 1.35) are popular too. Both palaces have educational purposes and provide catering services.

Case Study Chatsworth

Chatsworth (Figure 1.36) is the stately home of the Duke and Duchess of Devonshire, although it is actually in Derbyshire.

Location

The Chatsworth Estate is in the Peak District National Park in Derbyshire. (National Parks are featured in Chapter 1.6.) Chatsworth is 10 km north of Matlock and just over 25 km from junction 29 on the M1.

Purpose

A historic house and estate, Chatsworth provides a range of leisure products and services. Visitors

▲ *Figure 1.36 Chatsworth House*

enjoy the grand architecture of the house — inside and out. Figure 1.37 shows the 'Painted Hall' inside Chatsworth. Guided tours and a guidebook support visitors' enjoyment. There is also a collection of art, sculpture, furniture and design. Fountains can be found in the gardens and there are gift shops and food and drink outlets. Visitors can walk in the surrounding park without payment. 'Park' is the word used to describe the extensive grounds of grass and trees that typically surround stately homes. There is also a farmyard. Chatsworth was used as a location for the 2005 feature film *Pride and Prejudice*.

Like the other nationally important visitor attractions mentioned in this chapter, Chatsworth is also a major tourist attraction. People from all over the UK and some incoming tourists from other countries visit Chatsworth.

▲ *Figure 1.37 The 'Painted Hall' at Chatsworth House*

Have a Go

Know and understand	Apply what you know	Investigate
1 a Design a poster to promote either LEGOLAND® Windsor or Chatsworth. **b** Explain why it is important for leisure facilities to have catering services.	**2** You are the education officer for a historic site other than Chatsworth. Make a short PowerPoint presentation to show to other GCSE students, explaining the purposes of the site.	**3** Research and write the script for a television report about the location, products and services of a UK theme park other than LEGOLAND® Windsor.

Chapter

1.4

Home-based leisure and leisure-time choices

People can use local and national leisure facilities, such as sports venues and visitor attractions, in their leisure time. They can also spend time on home-based leisure activities. People make choices from a range of leisure activities.

Home-based leisure

Although home-based leisure activities are those that people enjoy in their own homes, the facilities that provide them are located away from the home, in:

- take-away restaurants
- DVD/video-rental shops
- bookshops
- libraries
- shops selling computer games

These facilities are usually found in town centres. Table 1.7 summarises the places in which take-away restaurants are often found. Similar location patterns affect other home-based leisure facilities, although there may be fewer examples of them in most towns.

▼ *Table 1.7 Locations of take-away restaurants*

The functions of home-based leisure facilities are often wider than is at first obvious. DVD/video-rental shops do more than rent DVDs

Distance from town centre →			
Town centre	**Suburbs and housing estates**	**Retail parks**	**Rural villages**
More restaurants	Fewer restaurants	Fast-food restaurants (take-away and drive-through)	Take-aways in larger villages
Fast-food chains and independent take-aways (e.g. kebab houses)	Home-delivery service		Home-delivery service
Cafés with take-away coffee and food	Independent small businesses such as Chinese and Indian take-aways and fish and chip shops		
Recent growth of espresso bars			

and videos and libraries do more than lend books. A DVD/video shop may offer DVDs and videos for sale and extra services like advance reservation and 24-hour drop-off points. They try to cater for the complete home-based leisure activity of spending a night in with a rented fim and often sell snacks, soft drinks and confectionery.

Practical scenario Investigating home-based leisure in a UK locality

Table 1.8 suggests how you could investigate home-based leisure facilities in a town using primary methods (your own investigations) and secondary methods (information from other sources).

One way of presenting the results of the investigation is to plot the locations of different types of facility on a street map, using a colour key.

Functions of individual examples can be noted in a written report to go alongside the map.

Take the investigation further

Look for patterns in the locations of each type of facility. How do their functions change with distance from the town centre?

▼ *Table 1.8 Research methods for home-based leisure locations*

Primary method	Secondary method
Brainstorm the locations and functions of home-based leisure facilities that you already know about in a town	Use the *Yellow Pages* and a street map to look up types of home-based leisure facility
Survey the location and functions of home-based leisure facilities in the town centre	Use the town guide and/or an internet search engine to look for examples in a named town

Leisure-time choices

People can choose either to stay at home or to go out for their leisure to local and national leisure facilities. The factors that affect these choices can be divided into two sets, as shown in Table 1.9.

Personal details/background	External factors
Age	Availability of local facilities
Culture	Availability of transport
Special needs	Interests
Household type	Fashion
Gender	Influence of family and friends
Social group	Money to spend

◀ *Table 1.9 Factors affecting leisure choice*

The first set of factors relates to personal details and background:

- **Age:** how old people are affects which leisure activities they choose. Children's play activities are obviously for children, but different age groups enjoy various activities. A soft-play facility in a local leisure centre is likely to be more suitable for preschool children than an adventure playground.

- **Culture**: young adults clubbing with their friends is an activity that is more acceptable to some cultural groups in the UK than to others.
- **Special needs**: if access is an issue, people may choose a facility with arrangements such as wheelchair ramps, lifts or hearing loops. In some older facilities, steps and stairs are a challenge for wheelchair users and people with children in pushchairs.
- **Household type**: some people live together as a family with children, others are single or live as a couple. This can affect what they choose to do. Parents with young children may have to make special arrangements (e.g. baby-sitting) before they can go out. Consequently, they may stay in for home-based leisure more often than single people and couples with no children.
- **Gender**: some leisure activities appeal more to one gender. For example, a water aerobics class at a leisure centre is likely to be attended mostly by women; some gyms admit only women.
- **Social group**: people's leisure choices can be influenced by the social class to which they belong. As with gender, people of all social classes can take part in any leisure activity. However, some activities are associated with certain social classes. For instance, more people from professional backgrounds (e.g. senior managers, doctors and lawyers) go to the theatre to see operas than play bingo.

The second set of factors that influences leisure choices concerns how people interact with the world around them, for example:

- **Availability of local facilities**: although people can choose to go to national leisure facilities, this could involve a long journey. Everyday leisure is done locally. What people do depends partly on what is available locally. In a city there may be a wider choice than in a rural area. London has a greater variety of local restaurants than rural Northumberland.
- **Availability of transport**: even home-based leisure depends on what transport is available. This is because people need to access facilities away from home to support such leisure activities. For example, choosing a take-away meal may depend on whether the restaurant delivers food.
- **Interests**: what is on offer from the leisure industry in a certain place will interest some people but not others. For example, the opening of a new squash club will attract local people who already play and some others who are interested by the new opportunity.
- **Fashion**: this leisure-choice factor means what is currently popular. Recent years have seen a fashion for Italian-style coffee. More

people have chosen to use cafés that sell espresso, latte and cappuccino coffee than before.

- **Influence of family and friends**: leisure activities are often done as part of a group. The choice of where to go and what to do is affected by the views of other people in the group. A teenager may be told to join the family at a relative's wedding reception or may choose a film because it is the one that friends want to see most.
- **Money**: leisure activities often cost money. There are travel costs to pay, as well as the price of the activity itself. People make choices on the basis of what leisure activities and facilities they can afford. Some may decide to travel to a theme park with a more exciting 'white-knuckle' ride because they have enough money. There is no need for them to settle for a possibly less exciting local alternative.

Figure 1.38 shows how some of the second set of factors (the external ones) affect the leisure choices made by 11-year-old schoolgirl Maren.

Figure 1.38 *Factors affecting Maren's leisure choices*

Have a Go

Know and understand	Apply what you know	Investigate
1 a Describe how any **two** personal factors can affect the leisure choices that people make. b Explain why transport availability is an important factor influencing people's leisure choices.	2 Evaluate the factors that determine your choice of leisure activities.	3 Interview different people. Find out which factors most affect their leisure choices.

Chapter

1.5

The travel and tourism industry

What is tourism?

Tourism is the visits that people make away from where they usually live and work. Tourists are people who travel from where they live in order to visit somewhere else. They do this for a variety of reasons that include:

- **leisure**: to enjoy their spare time, maybe on a short break or a holiday
- **business**: as part of their work, perhaps to attend a meeting or a conference
- **visiting friends or relatives**: this is called VFR tourism

There is more to tourism than just leisure tourism, and more to leisure tourism than just going on holiday. As well as holidays, leisure tourism can involve:

- sightseeing (e.g. viewing famous buildings, monuments or natural features such as waterfalls and volcanoes)
- visiting a tourist attraction (e.g. a theme park or historic site)
- going to a sports event either to watch (spectate) or to take part

Tourism involves at least one night spent away from home. Tourists are away from home only temporarily — they intend to return home after their trip is finished. Tourism differs from leisure because it involves travel *away* from the local area, whereas leisure can be enjoyed locally or away from home. Figure 1.39 shows the differences and similarities between leisure and tourism.

Because tourism involves being somewhere else, travel is its partner. Tourists travel to their destinations by air, road,

▼ **Figure 1.39**
Leisure versus tourism

Leisure
Leisure activities near home

Leisure activities away from home

Tourism
Business tourism
VFR

Neither:
Working at usual place/near home
Sleeping
Seeing to life's essentials (like food shopping)

rail and sea. The travel and tourism industry is the set of organisations that provides products and services for people at their destinations and help them to get there.

Key components of the travel and tourism industry

The travel and tourism industry is made up of parts called components. Each major (key) component includes organisations that provide a certain set of products and services. The key components of the travel and tourism industry are:

- travel agents
- tour operators
- tourist information and guiding services
- online travel services
- accommodation and catering
- attractions
- transportation

Travel agents

Travel agents are organisations that book travel and holidays for their customers. They are typically shops (Figure 1.40) located in town centres and so are often called high-street travel agents. Other travel agencies can be found in suburban shopping parades. Travel agents sell the products of other organisations such as:

- transport providers (e.g. airlines and train operators)
- tour operators

Travel agents are usually commercial organisations, for example Thomas Cook, Going Places and Travelcare.

▶ **Figure 1.40**
A high-street travel agency

Publishing Pictures

Recently, travel agents have undergone changes in:

- **Location**: more travel agents are now found outside town centres in places such as hypermarkets and out-of-town shopping malls.
- **Technology**: computers are now important in the day-to-day work of travel-agency staff. Someone who works in a travel agency, advising customers about holidays and making bookings for them, is called a travel consultant. They use special Viewdata software, which is a kind of teletext. Figure 1.41 shows a Viewdata screen.
- **Brands**: the name above the shop door is the travel agent's brand. Thomas Cook and Travelcare are examples of travel agents' brands. In today's travel and tourism industry, agents and tour operators are often parts of bigger travel companies. Thomson is both a tour operator and a travel agent with its own shops on the high street.

▼ **Figure 1.41**
Viewdata screen

Travel agents can arrange foreign currency for tourists. This is an additional service that they offer in order to save the customer from having to go elsewhere for their euros, US dollars and other currencies. Travel agents provide this customer service so that their clients are more likely to feel fully satisfied and come back again to book their next trip. Post offices, banks and specialist bureaux de change (usually found in airports and on board international ferries) can also change money for tourists.

Tour operators

Tour operators are businesses that arrange trips, including package holidays. A package holiday is a holiday that has been put together (packaged) from several elements. Typically, a package holiday abroad consists of:

- air travel from the UK to a gateway airport
- transfer from the airport to accommodation in a hotel or self-catering apartment
- accommodation
- transfer back to the airport and flight back to the UK

Holiday types, including package holidays, are explained in more detail later in this chapter.

Tour operators sell trips either through travel agents or directly to the customer. Companies such as Thomson have brochures that feature their holidays. The brochures are available in travel agencies and customers can pick a holiday from them and book it with the help of a travel consultant. Thomson brochures are not only available in Thomson agencies — other travel agents stock them too.

Direct selling means that the tour operator deals with the customer, missing out the travel agent. Direct Holidays is an example of a tour operator that delivers its brochures to customers' homes. To book a holiday, customers telephone Direct Holidays or use the internet. As the internet has become more popular, more tour operators have set up websites, even if they supply brochures to travel agents as well.

Coach companies are often tour operators too. As well as providing travel, they organise holidays and excursions that include accommodation or admission to an attraction. These companies can be large national operators such as National Express and Shearing or smaller, independent, local companies.

Tourist information and guiding services

Organisations that belong to this key component of the travel and tourism industry help tourists to find out what they need to know. It includes people who show tourists around destinations and facilities (guides). Examples include tourist information centres (TICs), which

▼ **Figure 1.42**
Tourist information centre

Publishing Pictures

are commonly found in towns and cities in the UK (Figure 1.42). Staff who work in TICs deal with enquiries from tourists who want details about the place they are visiting and can often help with transport and finding somewhere to stay. TICs stock leaflets and other tourist literature — some free and some for sale. They often have information about other destinations, as well as the locality in which they are situated.

Blue Badge guides (Figure 1.43) are qualified guides who show tourists around destinations in the UK. Their blue badges signify that they are knowledgeable and recognised travel professionals who can be trusted.

Many tourist attractions, especially historic sites, have their own guides. They are often volunteers or paid employees of the attraction.

www.visitcambridge.org

◀ *Figure 1.43*
A Blue Badge
guide with tourists
in Cambridge

Online travel services

Any help for tourist customers that can be accessed via the internet is
an online travel service. Such services include:

- online booking
- destination information
- travel updates
- databases used by the travel and tourism industry

Examples of online bookers include Expedia and Travelocity.
Customers can log on to the websites of these companies to find out
about travel (including air flights), accommodation (mostly hotels),
car hire and package deals. Customers can make their own bookings
online and pay by credit or debit card. An online booker that sells a
flight to a tourist acts as an online travel agency.

Destinations in the UK and abroad often have their own websites so
that customers can find out about them. The websites also market the
services of travel and tourism providers in the destination. Figure 1.44
is adapted from an extract of the Visit Cambridge website
(**www.visitcambridge.org**). Each of the links on the web page allows the
user to connect with travel and tourism providers that sell products
and services.

Visit Cambridge...Be Inspired

Email Newsletter   Send Page

Cambridge is a wonderful fusion of the everyday and the extraordinary, a living city that has shaped history, that today reflects the best of historic and contemporary life and is continuing to make its mark on the future.

Click here for Cambridge Visitor Information Centre details

Even if you have never visited Cambridge, it has still touched your life as the place that inspired Darwin, Newton, AA Milne, Wordsworth, John Cleese, Graham Chapman, Eric Idle and Stephen Hawking. Today it is inspiring thousands of Cambridge students and leads the way in new and emerging technology.

Short Breaks from £39

Stay. Relax. Be Inspired on a Cambridge Short Break. With a simple phone call we do the hard work for you.
Tel: 01223 457581 for more info »

Visitor Card for £2.50

Would you like to save money, whilst still enjoying the very best that Cambridge has to offer? The official Visitor Card provides exclusive offers & discounts in shops, restaurants, attractions and on guided tours of the city.
Click here for Visitor Card information »

3 Diamonds for Lynwood House

Lynwood House ideal for the business or tourist visiting our beautiful city, just a ten minute walk from the city centre, bt openzone internet available, rooms decorated in a contemporary style, enjoy our free range organic eggs and milk with your full English breakfast in our recently refurbished dining room.
More info on Lynwood House »

MP3 walking tours of the city

Don't fancy following a guided tour? Then try a Tourist Tracks MP3 walking tour of the city and see all the sights at your own pace. Our tours can be downloaded to your computer and are available on CD via mail order, or you can hire a pre-loaded MP3 player at the Tourist Information Centre.
Click here for more information »

Bedford Lodge Hotel

Set in three acres of secluded gardens, only 20 minutes from the centre of Cambridge. The hotel is a striking combination of classical and modern styles.
For further information on Bedford Lodge Click Here »

Watch video tours of Cambridge

Sample the unique atmosphere of Cambridge, with video tours from UK Tourist TV. Experience the picturesque Quayside, punting along the College Backs, & the beautiful Cambridgeshire countryside.
Look before you book »

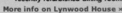

▲ *Figure 1.44*
Part of the Visit Cambridge website

Accommodation and catering

Tourists stay away from home temporarily, so restaurants are travel and tourism facilities only when they are linked to accommodation (e.g. a restaurant in a hotel). Types of accommodation include:

- hotels and guesthouses
- inns
- bed and breakfasts
- self-catering
- caravans and campsites

A variety of accommodation types can be found in UK tourist destinations such as seaside towns and cities. The Visit Cambridge website is one way of finding out about and contacting accommodation providers in Cambridge. Many UK towns and cities (not just resorts) publish town guides, which provide listings of available accommodation.

Attractions

Facilities that appeal to tourists in their destination (or while they are travelling) include visitor attractions such as:

- theme parks (e.g. Alton Towers)

- historic sites (e.g. Stonehenge)
- sights like the London Eye

Major visitor attractions in the UK are described in Chapter 1.3. As nationally important attractions, they draw tourist customers (people from outside the local area), as well as local leisure customers. Tourists who stay in London and ride on the London Eye are enjoying a leisure activity and are involved in tourism. This is because they are having fun in their spare time (leisure) and have travelled to London to stay away from home for a short period (tourism).

Transportation

Tourists need transportation to travel from home to their destinations. They may also need to travel within the destination. Organisations belonging to this key component include:

- airlines (e.g. British Airways and easyJet)
- ferry companies (e.g. P&O)
- coach companies (e.g. Shearing and Wallace Arnold)
- train operators (e.g. GNER and Virgin Trains)
- car-hire firms (e.g. Avis and Hertz)
- taxi operators

Means of travel are discussed in more detail later in this chapter.

Practical scenario — Investigating travel and tourism facilities in a UK locality

In any area in the UK there are examples of travel and tourism facilities that belong to the different key components of the industry. The locations of the travel and tourism facilities in your local town and the products and services that they provide can be investigated as described below.

1 Mark the locations of travel and tourism facilities on a street map of the town centre. Facilities could include travel agents, the tourist information centre (or the information desk in the library), the railway station, hotels and tourist attractions. Indicate to which key component each facility belongs using a key.

Make your map by brainstorming what you already know, surveying the town centre and using the town guide and *Yellow Pages*. You can also ask other people for information to help you.

Figure 1.45 shows Darlington town centre as an example. Darlington was also used as an example of the leisure industry in a locality in Chapter 1.1.

2 Use similar methods to research information so that you can annotate your map with examples of products and services offered by the facilities.

3 Illustrate your work with photographs or cuttings from promotional materials. You could present your work as a wall chart.

4 Analyse the travel and tourism facilities shown. Which components have more facilities? Why? Are there gaps in what is provided? What are they? Suggest reasons for these gaps.

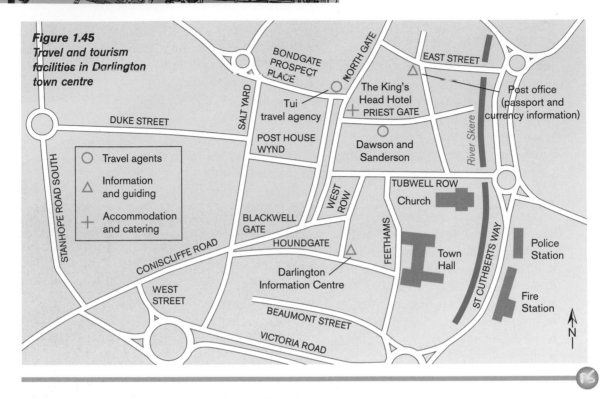

Figure 1.45
Travel and tourism facilities in Darlington town centre

Types of holiday

Holidays are trips made by leisure tourists. They are tourism for fun — not business tourism. There are different types of holiday.

Package holidays and independent travel

Package holidays include transport to a destination and accommodation there. Tour operators combine the two elements of transport and accommodation into one product, which can be sold to tourists either directly or through a travel agent. Figure 1.46 shows a package holiday from a tour operator's brochure.

Independent travellers make their own travel and accommodation bookings separately. They can use a travel agent or online booker to arrange the different elements, but they do not buy the holiday as a complete package.

Package holidays are often taken alongside other customers of the same tour operator. UK package holidaymakers could fly to Mallorca on the same aeroplane as other customers of the tour operator. The tour operator's resort representative may meet them all at Palma airport. Transfers to resorts such as Alcúdia could then be shared. The holidaymakers may find that they are staying in the same hotel as

ITALY Bay of Naples

8 Days Explore historic Campania, visiting Naples, Vesuvius, Capri & Pompeii (Itinerary Ref: CP)

Day 1	Fly to Naples
2	Naples; Visit to Vesuvius & Herculaneum
3	Free morning; boat to Capri
4	Capri; Blue Grotto; free afternoon
5	Free morning; boat to Sorrento
6/7	Sorrento; visit to Pompeii; free day for optional walks & excursions
8	Fly to London

ON THE WAY...

- Buried Pompeii
- Island of Capri
- Climb Mount Vesuvius

Walking, Relaxation & Discovery

This trip has it all. Enjoy various day walks including a climb to the top of the legendary volcanic crater — Vesuvius. For a cultural experience you'll wander the ancient Roman sites at Herculaneum and Pompeii. If you are also looking for relaxation the picturesque Bay of Naples, Capri Island and Sorrento Peninsula have a wonderful laid-back atmosphere.

some of the people on the flight. This is less likely to happen with independent travellers.

Domestic in-bound and out-bound tourism

- **Domestic tourism** is when a British tourist takes a trip inside the UK. Any tourists holidaying inside their own country take part in domestic tourism.
- **In-bound tourism** to the UK involves travellers from another country visiting the UK for a short period. They come into the UK for their trip.
- **Out-bound holidays** are taken by British people who travel abroad. They leave the UK for their holiday.

Short-haul and long-haul flights

Some holidays involve short-haul flights. From the UK, this is an aeroplane journey to another country in Europe or the Mediterranean. A flight to Spain or Greece is a short-haul flight, as is one to Cyprus or Malta. North African destinations and those in Israel and Turkey are not in Europe but are close enough to the

▲ **Figure 1.46**
Extract from a tour operator's brochure

Mediterranean Sea to be called short-haul. Figure 1.47 shows the short-haul destinations zone.

Long-haul flights from the UK go to places outside Europe and the Mediterranean. Destinations in North America, the Caribbean, Australia and the Far East are reached by long-haul flights.

Holidays involving short-haul flights differ from those with long-haul flights in other ways too:

- Long-haul-flight holidays tend to be more expensive and last longer.
- Short-haul flights are more likely to be operated by budget airlines (e.g. easyJet).
- Long-haul flights are more likely to involve a stop for refuelling and to be on larger aeroplanes such as jumbo and wide-bodied jets.

Special-interest holidays

People take special-interest holidays when they want to engage in activities such as:

- skiing
- walking
- sailing
- outdoor pursuits

- painting
- architecture
- attending the Olympic Games

▼ *Figure 1.47*
Short-haul
destinations

UK

Short-haul destinations

Specialist tour operators provide tours and package holidays to cater for such interests.

Short breaks

Short breaks are holidays that are less than a week long but involve at least one overnight stay. They are often taken in addition to a tourist's main holiday. City breaks have become particularly popular and some tour operators have brochures just for the city-break market. Budget airlines like easyJet and Jet2 have helped the growth of outbound tourism from the UK to cities such as Barcelona, Paris, Rome and Prague by offering cheaper flights to these destinations. Short skiing breaks have also increased in popularity recently for similar reasons.

Domestic short breaks in the UK are also popular. A short break in a UK resort, National Park or tourist town or city is often a shorter second holiday that supplements a tourist's longer main holiday abroad.

Methods of travel

Tourists can travel to and around destinations by the following means of transport:

- air
- rail
- sea
- road (bus, coach, car, taxi)

The relative merits of these different travel methods are listed in Table 1.10.

The most suitable method of travel depends on who is travelling and where the journey starts and finishes. For instance, a family with small children may find it convenient to use the car because they need only to pay for fuel (and not for separate tickets), they can start and end the journey exactly where they want (stopping on the way where they like) and they can transport their luggage easily.

A business tourist travelling to a meeting in central London may find it convenient to take the train because the journey ends in the heart of the city and is not affected by traffic jams. Such a business tourist might find that driving to and from the nearest railway station at the beginning and end of the day is the most convenient way to link home and train.

Figure 1.48 shows the locations of major international airports, ferry ports and motorways in the UK.

Method of travel	Relative merits		
	Cost	**Convenience**	**Availability**
Air	Traditionally expensive, but fares have fallen with the growth of budget airlines	Airports are distant from town centres but have good parking	More flights now that fares are lower More regional airports have services
Rail	Full fares can be expensive compared to coach travel Railcards and advance booking have reduced some ticket prices	Railway stations are usually in town centres	Larger cities have express services Smaller towns might have fewer trains
Sea	Cabins cost more Used to be cheaper than air, but now flights are more competitive	Drive-on ferries are good for car users Fewer services now because of budget airlines and the Channel Tunnel	Frequently used for crossing the English Channel Can become booked up at peak times
Road	People with their own cars need to buy just the fuel Coach and bus tickets are usually cheaper than rail and air	Flexible for car owners who are not restricted by timetables and can drive directly from home to their destination Coach stations are located in main town centres	Always available to those who have their own cars

▲ **Table 1.10**
Relative merits of travel methods

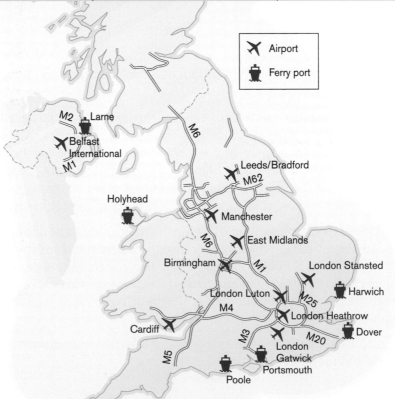

▶ **Figure 1.48**
Major UK airports, ferry ports and motorways

Have a Go

Know and understand	Apply what you know	Investigate
1 a Make a chart showing named organisations belonging to each of the key components of travel and tourism. **b** Describe the differences between: **i** travel agents and tour operators **ii** in-bound and out-bound tourism	**2 a** Use Table 1.10 to help you to recommend methods of travel for: **i** an elderly person travelling alone from London to Belfast **ii** a group of teenage friends travelling between London and Manchester **b** Explain the reasons for your recommendations.	**3 a** Research the travel options for a family of one adult and two preschool children leaving Manchester to travel to London Gatwick to catch a short-haul flight abroad. **b** Analyse the options and make a justified recommendation for them.

Chapter 1.6

UK tourism destinations

The places that tourists visit are destinations. Domestic tourists (from the UK) and in-bound tourists (from abroad) travel to destinations in the UK.

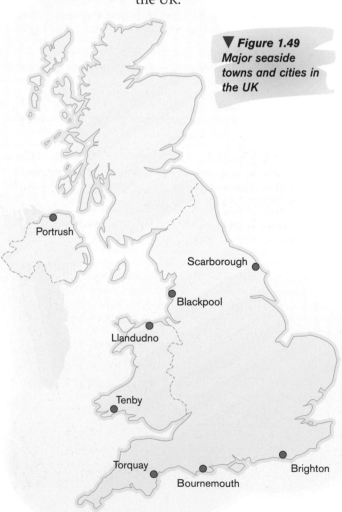

▼ *Figure 1.49 Major seaside towns and cities in the UK*

Types of destination

Examples of tourist destinations in the UK are:

- coastal areas (e.g. seaside resorts and Heritage Coasts)
- countryside areas
- tourist towns and cities
- visitor attractions (e.g. sporting venues, theme parks and places of historic interest)

Coastal areas

Coastal areas include seaside resorts: towns and cities on the coast that are important for tourism, such as Scarborough, Bournemouth, Blackpool and Brighton. Among the facilities available at UK resorts are beaches, promenades, amusement arcades, fairgrounds, piers, parks and landscaped gardens, hotels, guesthouses and self-catering apartments. The locations of some of the UK's main seaside towns and cities are shown in Figure 1.49.

CaseStudy Bournemouth

Location

Figure 1.50 shows the location of Bournemouth in the UK. It is a seaside resort in Dorset on the south coast of England. Bournemouth is about 30 km west of Southampton and about 150 km from London.

Main transport routes

The principal transport routes that tourists can use to visit Bournemouth are shown in Figure 1.50. The main road into Bournemouth is the A338, which branches south from the A31 just west of Ringwood. Drivers from London can follow the M3 southwest to Eastleigh near Southampton. The M27 links Eastleigh to the A31.

Bournemouth is on the railway line between Southampton and Dorchester. Passengers from London can take a train to Bournemouth from London Waterloo station.

Budget airlines that operate from Bournemouth include Ryanair, Jet2.com and Thomsonfly. Southampton Airport is a nearby alternative.

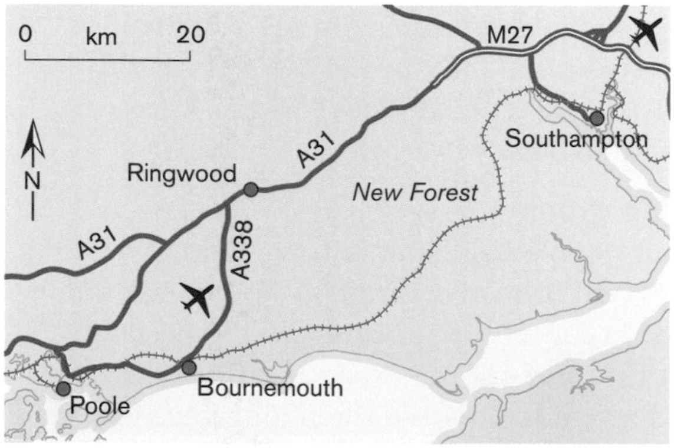

Major features

The beaches at Bournemouth are long, sweeping and sandy (Figure 1.51). Not all beaches on the south coast of England are sandy — some have shingle. In Bournemouth there are 11 km of golden sand. There are smoke-free beach zones as well as glass- and dog-free beaches. These are attractive to some families with small children. The sea is clean and Bournemouth has a Blue Flag award for the cleanliness of its shore.

Amusements can be found at Bournemouth Pier and Neptune Arcade, and there is bingo at Happylands near the West Cliff's lift, which suits some more elderly tourists. This group is among those types of tourist who enjoy cruises along the coast on one of the Dorset Belle boats.

▲ *Figure 1.50 Transport routes to Bournemouth*

*Figure 1.51
Bournemouth beach*

Brian Pickering; Eye Ubiquitous/CORBIS

The Oceanarium aquarium next to Bournemouth Pier has displays of marine life from environments around the world. It is a good wet-weather attraction for families with children.

There is a lot of green space in Bournemouth. Its public parks and gardens are a major attraction for some tourists.

On the East Cliff Promenade is the Russell-Cotes Art Gallery and Museum. This attracts visitors interested in the Victorian period, when Bournemouth was at its peak as a holiday resort.

Accommodation

There are more than 400 places to stay in the Bournemouth area, ranging from small guesthouses (e.g. the Sea Dene) to the grand Royal Bath Hotel, which has its own leisure complex with a swimming pool.

Heritage Coasts are special parts of the UK coastline. The government's Countryside Agency works with local authorities in England to look after these beautiful stretches of coastline. In Wales, the Countryside Council for Wales does the same job. There are over 40 Heritage Coasts in England and Wales, which add up to over 1,000 km of coastline. They are looked after to allow tourists to enjoy the landscape without damaging it for the future. This is sustainable management, which is explained more fully in the last part of this chapter. Most Heritage Coasts are parts of National Parks or Areas of Outstanding Natural Beauty (see below).

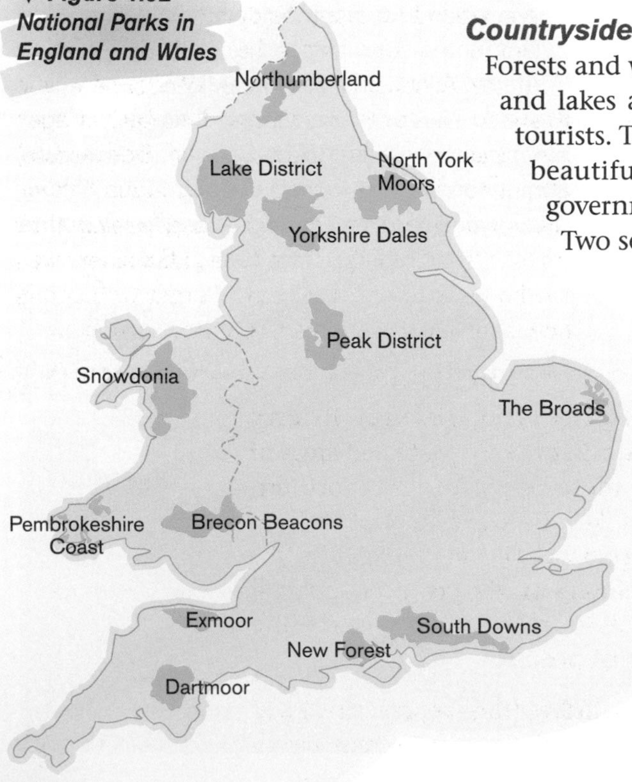

Countryside areas

Forests and woodlands, mountainous areas, rivers and lakes and attractive farmland all appeal to tourists. To conserve the landscape of especially beautiful and popular destinations, the government has marked them for protection. Two sets of these designated areas are:

- National Parks
- Areas of Outstanding Natural Beauty (AONBs)

National Parks are legally protected. They are large areas of countryside that have beautiful, often quite wild, scenery. Their wildlife and heritage make them particularly worth visiting and protecting. The National Parks of England and Wales attract over 110 million visitors a year. Figure 1.52 shows the locations of the National Parks of England and Wales.

▼ **Figure 1.52 National Parks in England and Wales**

Northumberland
Lake District
North York Moors
Yorkshire Dales
Peak District
Snowdonia
The Broads
Pembrokeshire Coast
Brecon Beacons
Exmoor
South Downs
New Forest
Dartmoor

Each National Park is controlled by a National Park Authority (NPA). The two main tasks of an NPA are:

■ to conserve the scenery, wildlife and heritage of the National Park
■ to promote enjoyment of the park by the public (local people and tourists)

 **The Lake District National Park**

Location and transport links

The Lake District National Park is in Cumbria in the northwest of England. The M6 runs just to the east of the National Park and is the main route from Manchester, just over 100 km to the south. The West Coast mainline railway from London Euston has stops to the east of the National Park at Oxenholme and Penrith. From Oxenholme, trains run into the Lake District itself, as far as Windermere.

Major features

There are 12 major lakes in the Lake District and numerous smaller ones, some of which are tiny tarns high up on the fells. The longest of the lakes is Windermere, which is 16.5 km long and approximately 1.5 km wide. It is popular with water-sports enthusiasts, especially at Bowness towards the southern end. A ferry service runs the length of Windermere from Bowness Pier; boats are also available for hire.

Like the other major lakes, Windermere is in a long and steep-sided valley that was eroded by a glacier. The hills (also known as 'fells') are largely open moorland and are popular with hill-walkers. Famous high fells, such as Helvellyn and Skiddaw, attract experienced walkers, but there are less challenging routes around the shores of the smaller lakes, Grasmere and Rydal Water.

The lakes in the northern part of the National Park, such as Ullswater, and the quieter, less visited western lakes of Ennerdale and Wastwater have more rugged scenery in comparison to the gentler slopes around southern Windermere.

The main towns of the Lake District National Park are Ambleside, Bowness/Windermere and Keswick. These towns and the stone-built villages like Grasmere and Rosthwaite (in Borrowdale) attract tourists who enjoy walking around them, visiting their shops and cafés and seeing their tourist attractions. Dove Cottage in Grasmere was the home of the poet William Wordsworth and is now a museum and a major popular attraction.

Figure 1.53 shows the **Areas of Outstanding Natural Beauty** (AONBs) in northern England. There are 30 of these protected areas of countryside in England alone, with more in Wales and Northern Ireland. The main difference between AONBs and National Parks is that AONBs do not have to create opportunities for recreation like National Park Authorities do. The development of recreation opportunities in AONBs is allowed as long as they help to conserve the scenery and fit in with the needs of local people.

Each AONB is managed by a committee that represents local authorities, landowners and local people. These committees try to

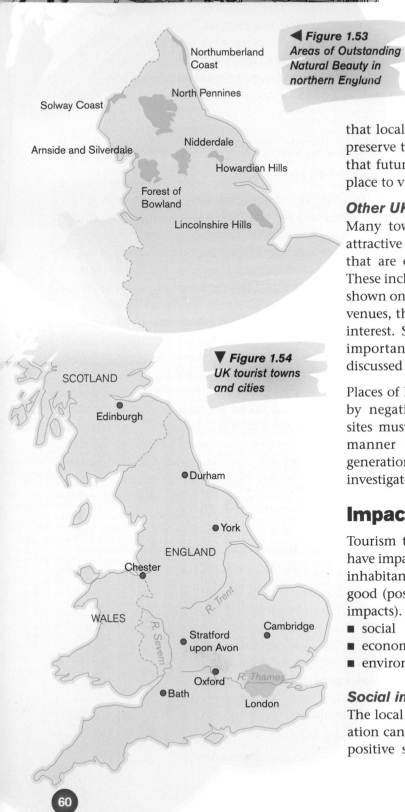

◀ **Figure 1.53**
Areas of Outstanding
Natural Beauty in
northern England

Northumberland Coast

North Pennines

Solway Coast

Arnside and Silverdale

Nidderdale

Howardian Hills

Forest of Bowland

Lincolnshire Hills

▼ **Figure 1.54**
UK tourist towns
and cities

SCOTLAND

Edinburgh

Durham

York

ENGLAND

Chester

R. Trent

WALES

R. Severn

Stratford upon Avon

Cambridge

Oxford

R. Thames

Bath

London

make sure that any development is done in a sustainable manner — any changes must not spoil the environment for local people and tourists in the future. It is important that local people can make a living and preserve their traditional way of life and that future tourists still have a beautiful place to visit.

Other UK tourist destinations

Many towns and cities in the UK are attractive to tourists, but there are some that are especially focused on tourism. These include the tourist towns and cities shown on Figure 1.54, which are sporting venues, theme parks or places of historic interest. Such attractions are nationally important leisure facilities and are discussed in Chapters 1.2 and 1.3.

Places of historic interest can be affected by negative impacts of tourism. Such sites must be managed in a sustainable manner to protect them for future generations. One example that you could investigate is Stonehenge.

Impacts of tourism

Tourism to any type of destination can have impacts on the place itself and on its inhabitants. The effects of tourism can be good (positive impacts) or bad (negative impacts). They can also be classified as:

- social
- economic
- environmental

Social impacts

The local community in a tourist destination can be affected by tourism. On the positive side, tourist destinations often have more leisure facilities than localities that have few tourists. For example, seaside resorts, such as Scarborough and Blackpool, have more hotels with function rooms to hire for events, such as wedding receptions, and more clubs and discos than other towns. In general, local people enjoy more varied leisure possibilities because of tourism. This is a social benefit.

Tourism can bring money into a destination and make the community more prosperous. The income raised in this way can be spent on improving social facilities that benefit local people.

However, tourism can have negative social impacts, which adversely affect local people. Seaside resorts and other tourist towns and cities attract retired people. This can unbalance the spread of ages of people that live there. Other negative social impacts that can affect tourist destinations include:

- friction and arguments between locals and tourists in bars and clubs
- disturbance to local people in seaside resorts caused by rowdy groups of tourists at night
- holiday homes bought by tourists in countryside areas leading to a housing shortage for local people, especially young couples, who then move out of the area
- changes in the provision of shops in smaller tourist towns to suit tourists rather than meet the everyday needs of local people

Economic impacts

Tourism can affect income and employment in a tourist destination. It brings jobs, for example in the key components of attractions and accommodation and catering. Tourism employees spend their money in other businesses in the destination and so they prosper too.

However, many tourism jobs, especially in seaside towns and cities, are seasonal. Employees in an attraction such as a water park have jobs for the summer season only. They may be unemployed and financially worse off for the rest of the year. This can depress the economy of the whole town out of season.

Environmental impacts

Positive environmental impacts can flow from the economic benefits for the area. The council can use local tax revenue to improve the environment by restoring public buildings and landscaping the town's parks and gardens. In order to attract tourists, facilities such as hotels and attractions need to have appealing grounds and frontages. This helps to improve the overall environment.

Environmental impacts of tourism can be negative too. The extra traffic created by tourists can cause noise and atmospheric pollution from vehicle exhausts, as well as being unsightly. Litter can be a problem in some of the busier parts of seaside resorts as it attracts seagulls, leading to noise and unsightly droppings. Noise at night, as partying tourists leave seaside nightclubs, is another form of pollution.

Sustainable tourism

Sustainable tourism means visiting a destination without damaging it for the future. High numbers of visitors can produce negative impacts on the local community, economy and environment. Their effects can last into the future. To stop this happening, tourism to destinations at risk is controlled. National Parks, Areas of Outstanding Natural Beauty (AONBs) and Heritage Coasts are examples of countryside destinations that are managed to minimise negative impacts and to ensure that any new developments will not harm the area — socially, economically or environmentally.

To make sure that destinations are developed sustainably, new tourism proposals are considered carefully by the local authorities. These include the committees and National Park Authorities that look after AONBs and National Parks. Approval is granted when the authorities are satisfied that the destination's future environment or the lives of its local people will not be adversely effected.

 The impact of tourism in the Lake District

Economic impacts

Figure 1.55 shows three bar graphs. Graph (a) illustrates how many millions of tourists visited Cumbria each year between 2000 and 2004. The Lake District is in the county of Cumbria, and it is the Cumbria Tourist Board's data that have been used to produce these graphs. Most tourists to Cumbria go to the Lake District. Graph (a) shows that the visitor numbers increased every year from 2001. In 2001 there was an outbreak of the cattle and sheep illness called foot-and-mouth disease. Many of the Lake District's fells and footpaths were closed to the public during this outbreak, so

visitor numbers fell. Rising visitor numbers since then suggest increasing impacts of tourism.

Graphs (b) and (c) show that the amount of money that tourists spent and the number of people who had jobs because of tourism both went up from 2001 to 2004. This suggests increased positive economic impacts of tourism — more money in the local economy and more jobs. On the downside, the drop in 2001 (because of foot-and-mouth disease) shows that the situation can change quickly and people can lose their jobs if something goes wrong. A negative economic impact of tourism is that if a destination relies on it too much, damage can be done when tourist numbers decrease suddenly.

The economy of the destination would be more sustainable if employment other than tourism jobs could be generated in the area. It is also important for organisations like the Cumbria Tourist Board to develop different sorts of tourism. If outdoor-activity tourism is affected by something like foot-and-mouth disease, then other types of tourism may be affected less. Indoor attractions in the towns then become important, such as the

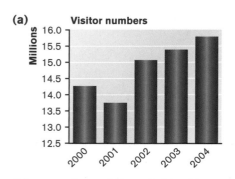

(a) Visitor numbers

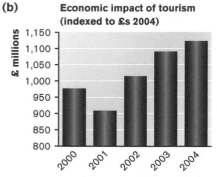

(b) Economic impact of tourism (indexed to £s 2004)

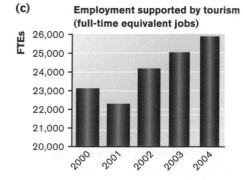

(c) Employment supported by tourism (full-time equivalent jobs)

▲ *Figure 1.55 Impacts of tourism in Cumbria*

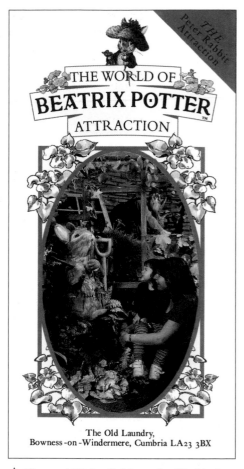

▲ *Figure 1.56 Leaflet from the World of Beatrix Potter visitor attraction in Cumbria*

World of Beatrix Potter museum in Bowness (Figure 1.56). A balance of different tourism types is more sustainable.

Environmental impacts

Figure 1.57a shows that footpath erosion is an environmental impact of tourism in the Lake District National Park. It is a problem faced by many countryside tourist destinations. You can see the footpath being repaired in Figure 1.57b. Part of the job of the National Park Authority (NPA) is to promote the Lake District to tourists, as the NPA wants to have more visitors, but the landscape must also be conserved.

Figure 1.57 ▲ (a) Footpath erosion and ▼ (b) repair in the Lake District National Park

The Lake District Tourism and Conservation Partnership promotes sustainable tourism by raising funds for conservation projects such as repairing worn footpaths. Figure 1.58 shows how much money this organisation raised between 2000 and 2005. The Youth Hostels Association (YHA) is one organisation that has helped to raise this money. It provides cheap accommodation for tourists throughout the National Park and beyond.

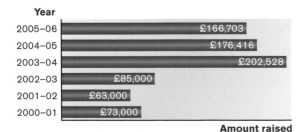

Year

Year	Amount raised
2005–06	£166,703
2004–05	£176,416
2003–04	£202,528
2002–03	£85,000
2001–02	£63,000
2000–01	£73,000

Amount raised

▲ **Figure 1.58 Money raised by the Lake District Tourism and Conservation Partnership**

Tourists staying at youth hostels are invited to help in three ways:
- making a small donation when booking their accommodation
- putting change in a collection box at the hostel
- paying for products and services at the hostel (e.g. postcards and cycle hire), which include a donation to the partnership in the price

At tourist facilities throughout the Lake District, visitors can pay a small voluntary surcharge to go towards the Lake District Tourism and Conservation Partnership's sustainable tourism projects.

Social impacts

Some villages in the Lake District have become highly tourist-oriented. An example is Hawkshead on the opposite side of Windermere to Bowness. Its shops are geared mostly towards the tourist trade rather than to the everyday needs of local people. The same is true of cafés and restaurants. Access for cars is more restricted than in a non-tourist village for safety reasons and in order to prevent congestion in the village centre. Careful management is needed to ensure that the everyday lives of local people are sustainable despite such impacts.

Limited access for tourist cars to the village centres is a start. In Hawkshead there is a separate car park just for local people, in addition to the large pay-and-display car park for visitors. This means that villagers always have space to park. It is important for the sustainability of the community that local people not directly involved in tourism for a living are able to carry on normal lives.

Tourism has positive social impacts in the Lake District too. Tourism jobs do not just bring money. Increased employment means that more local people can stay in the village and raise families there. There is still a village school in Hawkshead.

There is an integrated transport system in the Lake District: buses and other methods of transport, such as trains and, for some of the lakes, ferries, are timetabled to make connections easier. In Borrowdale valley the bus service is used and partly paid for by tourists. This means that residents of Rosthwaite, for instance, have a local bus despite the remoteness of their village.

Have a Go

Know and understand	Apply what you know	Investigate
1 a Design an information leaflet about a tourism destination. Include: • where it is • what it offers tourists • the main transport routes **b** Recommend a tourism destination for an elderly couple. Justify your choice.	**2 a** Compile a case study about a seaside town other than Bournemouth. **b** For a tourist destination, other than the Lake District: **i** Describe positive and negative economic, social and environmental tourism impacts. **ii** Suggest ways of developing the destination sustainably.	**3** Research an Area of Outstanding Natural Beauty close to you in order to give a presentation. The websites of the Countryside Agency (in England) (**www.countryside.gov.uk**), Countryside Council for Wales (**www.ccw.gov.uk**) or Environment and Heritage Service Northern Ireland (**www.ehsni.gov.uk**) are good starting points.

Combining leisure and tourism

The leisure industry and the travel and tourism industry are distinct sectors of the economy, but there are a lot of links between them. These links are related to the common characteristics of the two industries:

- key components
- customers
- facilities

Key component links

The leisure and the travel and tourism industries are each made up of parts called key components, which are summarised in Table 1.11. Details of these components are given in Chapters 1.1 and 1.5.

▶ *Table 1.11 Key components of the leisure and travel and tourism industries*

Leisure	Travel and tourism
Sport and physical recreation	Travel agents
Arts and entertainment	Tour operators
Countryside recreation	Tourist information and guiding services
Home-based leisure	Online travel services
Children's play activities	Accommodation and catering
Visitor attractions	Attractions
Catering	Transportation

The lists in Table 1.11 suggest that there is some overlap between the key components. Visitor attractions of the leisure industry that have tourist customers belong to the travel and tourism industry as well. This applies to the national leisure facilities that are also visitor attractions. Theme parks, historic sites, facilities such as the London Eye, zoos, safari parks, museums and galleries of more than local importance are also tourist attractions. This is because they are visitor attractions with some customers who have travelled away from their normal homes, spending at least one night somewhere else. These customers are tourists. Alton Towers, LEGOLAND®, Bristol Zoo, Chatsworth and Stonehenge are examples of this key component link between leisure and tourism.

Catering overlaps between the two industries to a limited extent. Catering facilities that are part of the travel and tourism industry are also leisure facilities. Hotel restaurants or cafés inside theme parks are examples of the key component link between the two industries. However, a take-away restaurant or a fast-food restaurant on a leisure park is not. These facilities serve local people first and foremost. Although they may have some customers who happen to be tourists, this is coincidental. Therefore, they are not parts of the travel and tourism industry.

Customer links

Figure 1.59 gives some examples of customer links between leisure and tourism. Each scenario involves customers of the leisure industry who are, at the same time, customers of the travel and tourism industry too.

In the first scenario (a), a family with children is visiting a theme park. This is a leisure activity because they are having fun in their spare time. The family has travelled to the area on a coach, as part of a short break, and is staying at a nearby hotel overnight. Travelling away from home combined with their overnight stay makes their visit to the theme park tourism too. The family is a customer of both the leisure and the travel and tourism industries.

The second scenario (b) shows football supporters who have travelled to watch an away match. Sport spectating is a leisure activity. Staying overnight in a city-centre hotel after the match turns the trip into tourism as well.

The final two scenarios in Figure 1.59 show two other customer links between leisure and tourism. In the third scenario (c), holidaymakers (tourists) are enjoying a water park at their destination. This is a leisure activity while they are staying away from home. The two industries share the holidaymakers' custom, which is the leisure–tourism link. The last scenario (d) shows members of the audience at a rock festival. Watching the band is a leisure activity in the arts and entertainment component. Camping at the festival (away from home) means the fans are on a travel and tourism trip too — another link between leisure and tourism.

▲ *Figure 1.59*
Scenarios involving
customer links

Facility links

Example 1

The tourist information centre (TIC) in a tourism destination offers a range of local information, such as details of accommodation and leisure facilities (restaurants, visitor attractions and theatres). Although the TIC is clearly part of the travel and tourism industry's information and guiding component, it also provides a service to leisure-industry facilities.

Example 2

Coach companies are commercial organisations that belong to the transportation key component of the travel and tourism industry. They often take their passengers to leisure facilities. For example, a coach could be organised to take youth-club members to a bowling alley in a leisure park. This means that the travel and tourism organisation is providing a service to leisure-industry customers, thus linking leisure and tourism.

Have a Go

1 Draw cartoon sketches to illustrate **two** scenarios that show links between leisure and tourism, other than those given in Figure 1.59.

2 Explain why **two** scenarios (other than those above) show links between leisure and tourism.

3 Research links:

a with tourism of a local leisure facility

b with leisure of a travel and tourism facility in your local area

Jobs in leisure and tourism

The leisure and the travel and tourism industries offer a wide range of jobs. Table 1.12 shows some examples of the work available in these sectors.

Leisure	Travel and tourism
Leisure assistant	Travel consultant
Fitness instructor	Conference organiser
Lifeguard	Coach driver
Ground-staff member	Air cabin crew
Park ranger	Tourist guide
Restaurant manager	Resort representative

▲ **Table 1.12** *Jobs in the leisure and tourism industries*

Jobs in leisure

Leisure assistants are employed in leisure centres to help customers make the most of the facilities on offer. **Fitness instructors** can work in leisure centres or health clubs. Their duties can include demonstrating the use of gym equipment, running aerobics classes and designing fitness programmes for customers. **Lifeguards** may be based at swimming pools, including those in leisure centres, or at seaside resorts on beaches. **Ground-staff members** may work at a sports venue such as a football or cricket stadium, undertaking duties such as preparing playing surfaces for matches. Alternatively, they may work at a theme park, where their duties, such as maintaining the tidiness of the theme park, bring them frequently into contact with customers.

Park rangers are outdoor workers in National Parks. They are concerned with ensuring that the park and its customers are properly cared for. **Restaurant managers** are in charge of the operation of a restaurant during their hours of duty. An important aspect of their work is to manage a team of people, including waiting staff who provide customer service to diners.

In the leisure industry (and the travel and tourism industry), jobs are available at different levels of seniority. A leisure assistant is a junior member of staff who reports to the leisure-centre manager. Leisure employees on higher grades expect to be better paid than colleagues on lower grades. Opportunities for promotion may exist for junior staff who are ambitious and work hard, so career progression is possible for school and college recruits to the industry. Entering the leisure industry at a higher (managerial) level requires additional qualifications from further or higher education.

Case Study Fitness instructor: a leisure-industry job

Figure 1.60 is an extract from a website advertisement that gives some details about working as a fitness instructor in a health club belonging to the leisure organisation LA Fitness. The advert outlines what fitness instructors who work for LA Fitness have to do and what the company looks for in new recruits.

REPS is the Register of Exercise Professionals, a database of qualified instructors. LA Fitness wants its instructors to have sufficient qualifications to be listed on the REPS at Level 2. This could be the National Vocational Qualification (NVQ) called 'Instructing in Exercise and Fitness'. The company also thinks that it is desirable for fitness instructors to have a Certificate in Exercise to Music (ETM).

Duties

The duties of an employee are the tasks that need to be completed and the responsibilities that have to be shouldered in the course of doing the job. For the LA Fitness instructor, these are listed under the heading 'What you will do' in Figure 1.60. One duty of the job holder is to take new health-club members through an induction (or introduction) process. This involves showing the new customer around, demonstrating the correct and safe use of equipment and helping to design a fitness programme.

Skills

Skills are what job holders are able to do. Listening carefully to people and communicating clearly with them are examples of relevant skills for a fitness instructor to have.

L·A FITNESS

Position: Fitness Instructor

Who we are:
LA Fitness is a leading operator of health and fitness clubs in the UK operating over 65 clubs throughout.

What you will do:
- Conduct new members' inductions.
- Support members achieving their 'real life' fitness goals.
- Ensure facilities are maintained to the highest standards at all times.
- Drive membership satisfaction, and ensure high membership retention.
- Ensure that targets set by managers are met.

What we are looking for:
- REPS level 2 qualified.
- Good knowledge of fitness procedures and fitness products.
- Customer service focused.
- Team Worker.
- Ideally ETM qualified and able to teach classes.

▲ *Figure 1.60 Details of a leisure job on the internet*

Personal qualities

Personal qualities are aspects of an employee's character. The skills of a job holder depend partly on their personal qualities. For example, the skill of listening carefully stems from the qualities of patience and caring. Specific qualities expected of a fitness instructor can be worked out from the 'What we are looking for' list in Figure 1.60. They include having a good memory for the fitness procedures and products knowledge that is expected by LA Fitness. Other requirements for the job include being a team player (someone who can work well with others), confidence (to be able to teach members), as well as customer-service qualities such as patience, cheerfulness, politeness and empathy with others.

Have a Go

Know and understand	Apply what you know	Investigate
1 Suggest why having customer-service qualities of: • patience • cheerfulness • politeness • empathy is important for a fitness instructor.	**2** Write a letter of application for the job advertised in Figure 1.60. Explain how you would suit LA Fitness's requirements.	**3** Research the duties, skills and personal qualities required for any one leisure-industry job.

Jobs in travel and tourism

Travel consultants work in travel agencies. They advise customers about travel arrangements and holidays and make bookings for them. A **conference organiser** could be based in a hotel. Larger hotels in cities are often used as venues for business meetings and conferences. The hotel's conference manager may need to coordinate several such meetings each day.

Coach drivers work in the transportation key component of the travel and tourism industry. On longer tours, the coach driver may also act as a tour guide. Members of the **air cabin crew** look after the welfare of passengers on flights and may work on domestic, short-haul or long-haul routes. Destinations and visitor attractions often have **tourist guides** to show customers around. Such guides may be employed or work as volunteers. Some qualified Blue Badge guides in the UK are self-employed.

Tour operators employ **resort representatives**. Working for a UK tour operator with out-bound tourist customers may mean that a resort representative needs to live and work abroad, at least during the main tourism season. Some resort representatives divide their year, working in a coastal Mediterranean resort in the summer and at a ski resort in the Alps in the winter.

Case Study · Resort representative: a travel and tourism job

Resort representatives are based in a tourism destination abroad. Their role is to look after the welfare of the tour-operating company's customers. They welcome customers to the resort and help them to enjoy their holiday, as well as sorting out any problems that might arise, such as if someone has an accident or there is a mix-up with the type of room a customer has been given by the hotel.

In Figure 1.61, a resort rep based in Chania, a resort on the Greek island of Crete, describes the skills and personal qualities that a good tour-operator's rep needs. The job involves providing customer service. Reps need to know about the holidays that customers have bought and about

the resort itself to help ensure that customers have enjoyable holidays. Topic 3 of this book is devoted to customer service in leisure and tourism.

Welcome meetings are held to explain to customers what is on offer at their hotel and in the resort. Reps use these meetings to promote excursions to customers as extras to their holiday. Selling these trips earns valuable commission for reps to add to their basic salary. Figure 1.62 gives details of an all-day coach tour for families organised by resort reps for customers on holiday in the Mallorcan resort of Alcúdia. Starting from the Hotel Pollensa Park in Port de Pollença, the trip includes a visit to Marineland in Palma Nova to see a dolphin show and then play crazy golf

To be a success in this job, you can't be a shrinking violet. You've got to love meeting new people and enjoy exploring new places. Reps need to get on well with people.

You need great selling skills because commission on trips that you run boosts your basic pay. You need loads of energy and enthusiasm as well as a calm attitude and patience. It gets pretty hectic at times, so a really positive attitude is important too.

Unexpected situations happen suddenly and you have to be able to sort them out.

I had a bit of French from school and that helped me learn a bit of Greek when I came to Crete. It's certainly a bonus if you do speak a second language.

Reps need self-confidence to build rapport with local hotel and facility people as well as with their customers.

Figure 1.61 What makes a good resort representative?

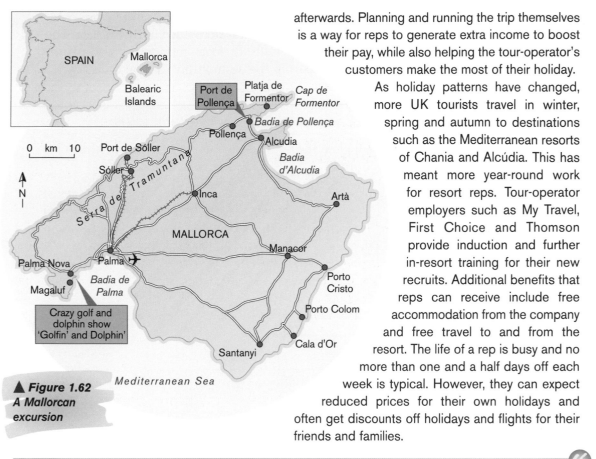

**▲ Figure 1.62
A Mallorcan
excursion**

afterwards. Planning and running the trip themselves is a way for reps to generate extra income to boost their pay, while also helping the tour-operator's customers make the most of their holiday.

As holiday patterns have changed, more UK tourists travel in winter, spring and autumn to destinations such as the Mediterranean resorts of Chania and Alcúdia. This has meant more year-round work for resort reps. Tour-operator employers such as My Travel, First Choice and Thomson provide induction and further in-resort training for their new recruits. Additional benefits that reps can receive include free accommodation from the company and free travel to and from the resort. The life of a rep is busy and no more than one and a half days off each week is typical. However, they can expect reduced prices for their own holidays and often get discounts off holidays and flights for their friends and families.

Summary of links between leisure and tourism

The first part of this chapter concerns links between the leisure and travel and tourism industries. A job holder in one industry may deal with customers of the other. For example, a park ranger in a National Park such as the Lake District may interact with tourists. Hotel reception employees work in the travel and tourism industry but may deal with local people who are leisure customers of the hotel.

For the two jobs featured in this chapter's case studies, the links between leisure and tourism are:

■ **Fitness instructor**: business tourists, for example, may take out a temporary membership at a health club while staying away from home. The fitness instructor may provide a service to them, carrying out the normal duties outlined in the case study.

■ **Resort representative**: tourist customers of the resort representative will want to enjoy leisure facilities provided in their resort. The rep could organise group visits to local restaurants and visitor attractions, which are part of the destination's leisure industry.

Have a Go

Know and understand	Apply what you know	Investigate
1 Explain why resort reps need the skills and personal qualities listed in Figure 1.61.	2 Write part of the script for a welcome meeting run by a resort rep to promote the trip in Figure 1.62.	3 Research a travel and tourism job other than that of a resort representative. a Describe the job holder's duties. b Explain the skills and personal qualities he/she needs.

Topic 2

Marketing in leisure and tourism

Chapter
2.1

What is marketing?

Leisure and tourism organisations are businesses that provide products and services for their customers. Marketing leisure and tourism is about making sure that customers know what products and services are on offer, that they want them and that they can access them.

Some leisure and tourism organisations are commercial (e.g. travel agents) — they aim to make a profit. For these companies, marketing is about ensuring that customers buy the products and services that they sell. Non-commercial organisations (e.g. leisure centres) provide a service to the public. Marketing for leisure centres involves attracting members of the public to use the facilities available.

Leisure and tourism organisations want customers to be satisfied with the products and services they receive, so that they return and also tell other people how good the organisation is. The organisation will then have more customers and make more money (if it is commercial). This is called the multiplier effect, because it increases customer numbers and raises profits.

Customers are satisfied if they are happy with:
- the quality of products and services
- the price

Marketing makes sure that the products customers receive are what they want and at prices they think are fair. It involves ensuring that products are:
- promoted so that customers know about them
- available in places that can customers can reach easily

Leisure and tourism organisations use four main marketing tools:
- target marketing
- market research
- marketing mix
- SWOT analysis

In this chapter, we look at target marketing and market research. In Chapter 2.2, we examine the marketing mix. SWOT analysis is explained in Chapter 2.3.

Leisure and tourism organisations use a wide range of promotional materials, including brochures, leaflets, flyers and advertisements.

Have a Go

Know and understand	Apply what you know	Investigate
1 a Explain what is meant by marketing. **b** Why do: **(i)** commercial and **(ii)** non-commercial leisure and tourism organisations market their products and services?	**2 a** Study Figures 2.12 and 2.13 (pages 95 and 96). Explain how each helps a leisure and tourism organisation to market its products and services. **b** Watch a television travel programme report on a tourist destination. Evaluate how critical the programme is of the destination shown.	**3 a** Collect a range of promotional materials used by different leisure and tourism organisations. **b** For one leisure and one tourism organisation, suggest how promotional material from your collection helps them to market their products and services.

Target marketing

Target marketing is a tool used by leisure and tourism organisations to ensure that customers can obtain their products and services easily. It is used to identify the different types of customers who most want the organisation's products and services. The organisation concentrates on aiming products and services at these target customer types. In this way, the company avoids wasting time, effort and money on promoting products and services to people who do not want them.

Each group of customers has different needs. For example, teenagers' requirements differ from those of retired people, as do those of sporty and less health-conscious people. These customer groups are called market segments, and the segments combine to make the leisure and tourism market: the whole set of customers for whom an organisation provides products and services. Leisure and tourism markets can be segmented in a number of ways according to:

■ **Age**: how old customers are affects the products and services that they want (or demand). Young children want to hire different films from a video-rental shop than those chosen by their parents. To keep both customer types satisfied, the shop must provide a range of films. National restaurant chains offer activities such as play areas and puzzles for children. This keeps younger customers occupied, which is also a service to their parents. Therefore, two age groups and the families market segment have been satisfied. This is part of marketing the restaurant. It means that customers are more likely to return to the restaurant and to tell other people about the service they received (the multiplier effect).

- **Gender**: male and female customers, even of similar ages, can have different leisure and tourism demands. Some local leisure centres and health clubs provide women-only gym facilities, often without a male equivalent. National recreation centres offer courses and coaching that are geared towards either men or women, particularly since many sports have separate male and female events and teams.

- **Social group**: customers from a higher income bracket, with more money to spend on leisure and tourism, are likely to have different demands from those of people with lower incomes. Professional people, such as senior managers, doctors and lawyers, may have different requirements to some working-class people. For example, on a national scale, tour operators try to cater for social groups by providing holidays to different destinations and with various grades of accommodation. Locally, leisure centres offer a range of activities that meet the needs of a range of social groups.

- **Lifestyle**: how people live their lives is connected to other factors such as their age and the social group to which they belong. However, people from the same age and social groups and of the same gender can still have different lifestyles. Home-based leisure such as computer gaming fits in more with some people's lifestyles than outdoor activities such as sport. Active, outdoor lifestyles form a separate market segment from indoor, passive lifestyles. Tour operators provide for the demands of active tourists by marketing holidays based around physical recreation such as skiing and walking.

- **Ethnicity**: people's cultural backgrounds can affect the leisure and tourism products and services they want. In large cities, some restaurants specialise in ethnic food. For example, a Turkish restaurant in London may cater for customers from a Turkish background as well as for people of other ethnicities who enjoy Turkish food or want to try something different. Travel agents in some inner-city neighbourhoods specialise in flights to destinations such as the Caribbean or south Asia. The local population in these cities includes a high proportion of people who originate from these parts of the world and wish to travel back on visits.

Target marketing is the marketing tool that leisure and tourism organisations use to provide the right products and services for their different customer groups. Managers of leisure and tourism facilities ask themselves who their customers are — to which of the market segments described above do the customers belong? The organisation can then decide which products and services to provide. These will be products and services for which there is a demand, at a price that the customers can afford to pay and that will be sufficient to cover the company's costs. Managers of commercial organisations need to know that the prices that customers can pay will be sufficient for the company to make a profit. If the price is too high for the market segment, customers will not pay and the organisation will not make money. The target for marketing products and services must be judged correctly. In Figure 2.1, a tour operator explains target marketing.

◄ *Figure 2.1*
A tour operator explains target marketing

We sell luxury villa holidays in the south of France to customers in the UK. When we started, we worked out who our customers were likely to be. They would be families rather then couples, quite well off, often professional, people who had been to France before, with some new to travelling there. There would be a mix of gender and no need to target any specific ethnic group.

Then, we worked out where we could advertise and how much we thought people would be willing to pay for a holiday in one of our villas. That had to be enough to ensure we made a profit.

Other market segments include:
- **New customers and existing customers**: it is important for any leisure and tourism organisation to market products and services to its existing customers in order to retain them for future business. However, an organisation may decide to target new clients in order to expand its operation.
- **Members and non-members**: some leisure organisations are clubs. Particular products and services may be aimed only at members,

but others could be marketed to the general public, perhaps with a view to attracting new people to join the club.

- **Local people and tourists**: in a tourism destination, a facility manager may need to be aware of the potential of the market segment of local people, as well as satisfying the demands of visitors. A seaside-resort hotel may be busy with tourists during the summer season but experience a fall in trade during the winter. Targeting business tourists could help to keep customers coming to the hotel for conferences, but marketing the hotel's products and services to local people for functions such as wedding receptions or for everyday use of its gym, restaurant and bar can be another way to keep money coming in.

- **Individual customers and groups**: marketing to larger groups of people, such as coach parties or business hospitality clients can increase the profits of leisure and tourism facilities. Some theme parks are keen to attract education groups from schools and colleges, for example. These groups tend to visit between Monday and Friday, during term time, when the park is likely to be quieter. At weekends and during the school holidays, family groups may form a larger segment of the theme park's market.

Case Study The Cumbria Tourist Board

The Cumbria Tourist Board promotes tourism to Cumbria — the most northwesterly county in England. Cumbria includes the Lake District National Park (see Chapter 1.6), which most tourists to Cumbria visit.

One way in which the Cumbria Tourist Board sets out to promote tourism to the county is by helping leisure and tourism organisations to identify their target markets. It advises four-star hotels in the Lake District to target affluent couples (with or without children), with high disposable incomes, in social groups A and B and living within a 160-km radius of the hotel. Such people are most likely to want to and be able to afford to stay in a hotel such as the four-star Low Wood Hotel (Figure 2.2) on the shore of Lake Windermere.

Hotels in the UK are classified using a star system. The more stars that a hotel is awarded, the more facilities it has. The maximum number of stars is five. A four-star hotel is usually a large and luxurious hotel.

People with high disposable incomes can afford to choose a hotel like the Low Wood Hotel. Most hotel rooms are twin or double rooms and so they are best suited to adults in pairs. Hotels tend to have fewer single rooms, which are more expensive per person than twin or double rooms. By targeting couples, hotels avoid wasting effort, time and money in trying to market single rooms, which do not bring in much business.

Social groups A and B contain professionals and senior managers. Social groups C and D refer to office, skilled and semi-skilled workers. Group E contains people without specialised skills and who are least likely to have high disposable incomes. Disposable income means the money left over after spending on life essentials such as food, housing, heating and clothes. Leisure and tourism spending comes out of people's disposable income.

Figure 2.2 Low Wood Hotel in Windermere

Low Wood Hotel, Lake Windermere/www.elh.co.uk

Have a Go

Know and understand	Apply what you know	Investigate
1 Make a table to show local and national examples of leisure and tourism facilities that target different market segments.	**2** For one leisure or one travel and tourism organisation: **a** Suggest market segments that it targets currently and that it could target. **b** Justify your answers.	**3** Prepare questions to ask in an interview with the manager of a leisure or tourism facility about the facility's target markets.

Customer profiling

Customer profiling involves identifying and describing the main customer types of a leisure and tourism organisation.

Kuoni is a major tour operator. Figure 2.3 shows the front cover of one of its travel brochures. Kuoni's target market has expanded substantially over the past decade. In the past, the company sought to attract a broad market, but most clients have traditionally come from the 45–54 age group due to the relatively luxurious and expensive nature of the Kuoni package-holiday product. Kuoni holidays appeal to

KUONI

JANUARY TO DECEMBER 2005

Tropical sun

THREE STAR HOTELS IN EXOTIC PLACES

KUONI

A World of Difference

www.kuoni.co.uk

◀ **Figure 2.3**
Front cover of a Kuoni travel brochure

empty-nesters (adults whose children have grown up and left home) and retired couples. However, there has been a recent change in the Kuoni customer profile with an increase in customers in their thirties and early forties. How can Kuoni use market research to find out how its customer profile has changed? One way to investigate customer profile is to compile a database of client information using completed booking forms. This database can be stored on a computer and then searched in order to build the customer profile.

Market research

Market research is the marketing tool that leisure and tourism organisations use to find out what their customers want. They do this in a variety of ways, including:

- postal surveys
- telephone questionnaires
- personal surveys
- observation
- internet research

▼ **Figure 2.4**
An evaluation form

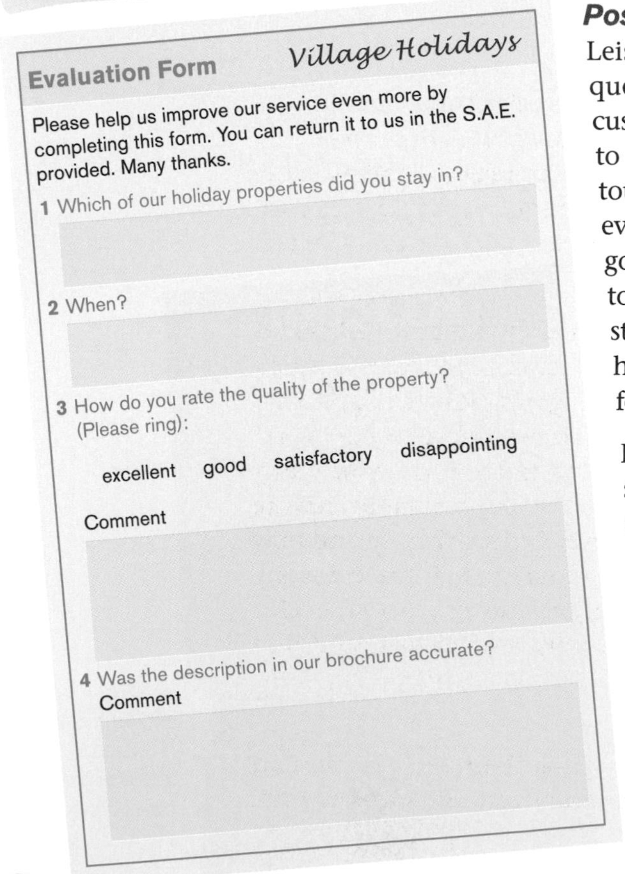

Evaluation Form   *Village Holidays*

Please help us improve our service even more by completing this form. You can return it to us in the S.A.E. provided. Many thanks.

1 Which of our holiday properties did you stay in?

2 When?

3 How do you rate the quality of the property? (Please ring):

excellent   good   satisfactory   disappointing

Comment

4 Was the description in our brochure accurate?
Comment

Postal surveys

Leisure and tourism organisations use questionnaires that new or existing customers complete in writing and send to the organisation in the post. Some tour operators send customers a blank evaluation form (Figure 2.4) before they go on holiday. To encourage customers to reply, the tour operator provides a stamped addressed envelope. After the holiday, the customer completes the form and posts it to the operator.

In the autumn, after the main tourist season is over, the tour operator looks at all the returned evaluation forms and works out the percentages of customers who were satisfied with each aspect of the service provided, as well as how many would like to see new products and services. As far as the tour operator is concerned, there are two main purposes to this market research:

- **Planning**: by collecting, analysing and evaluating postal-survey responses, the tour operator can plan which products and services to provide the following year, whether to make any changes and how much customers may be willing to pay. The market segments to be targeted can also be planned using the results of the postal survey.
- **Customer service**: asking customers to complete a postal survey at their leisure makes them feel that their opinions are valued and will make a difference to the holidays that the tour operator organises.

Both planning and customer service are marketing purposes, because they are about making sure that the right *products* and services are provided and *promoted* to the right customer types at the right *price* and in the right *place* — the 4 Ps:

- product (what is offered)
- price (how much is charged)
- promotion (how customers are told about the product)
- place (where the product can be accessed by the customer)

The blend of these four marketing ingredients is known as the marketing mix, which is the subject of Chapter 2.2.

Telephone questionnaires

Market research can be carried out on the telephone. Leisure and tourism organisations contact existing and potential customers by telephone. Potential customers are people who may use the products and services of a leisure and tourism organisation, but have not yet done so. Existing customers are sometimes referred to as actual customers.

Telephone questionnaires can be carried out by specialist organisations, such as Gallup or MORI, on behalf of leisure and tourism organisations. Sometimes leisure and tourism organisations use data that these polling companies have gathered about people's lifestyles as part of a more general survey. This includes information on how many people from different market segments have particular leisure interests, how far they are prepared to travel for their leisure and how much money they have to spend on it. A national leisure company considering opening a new bowling alley, multiplex cinema, health and fitness club, video-rental shop or family restaurant would find such data useful.

Personal surveys

Questionnaires that involve face-to-face contact between a leisure and tourism organisation's representative and its customers are personal

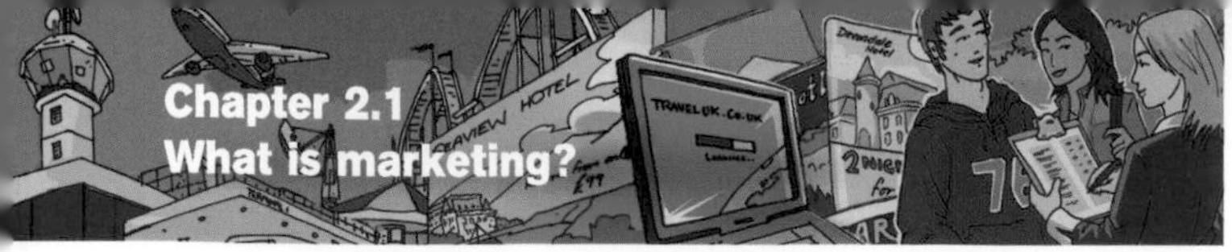

surveys. They may be carried out by interview or the customer can be given a form to complete that is collected later. The International Passenger Survey is an example. Airline passengers are interviewed at airports about their journeys. The results are compiled and studied to help companies plan the provision of products and services to their customers. Train operators survey customers during train journeys. A member of staff walks along the train and leaves questionnaire forms with a sample of passengers. These customers are asked to complete the forms during their journeys. The survey forms are collected later.

Sampling means that only some people are surveyed rather than everyone. Sometimes it may be appropriate for leisure and tourism organisations to give every customer the opportunity to take part in market research. The tour operator in Figure 2.4 sends postal-survey forms to everyone who makes a booking. Customer comment cards and evaluation forms — like the one used by the Blue Planet Aquarium (Figure 2.5) are common. Organisations know that some customers will complete survey questionnaires and some will not. In the end, a sample will have been taken. Telephoning or interviewing each customer personally is neither practical nor desirable.

Personal surveys need to be carried out tactfully. Leisure and tourism organisations do not want their customers to feel that they cannot relax and enjoy themselves because they have a form to complete.

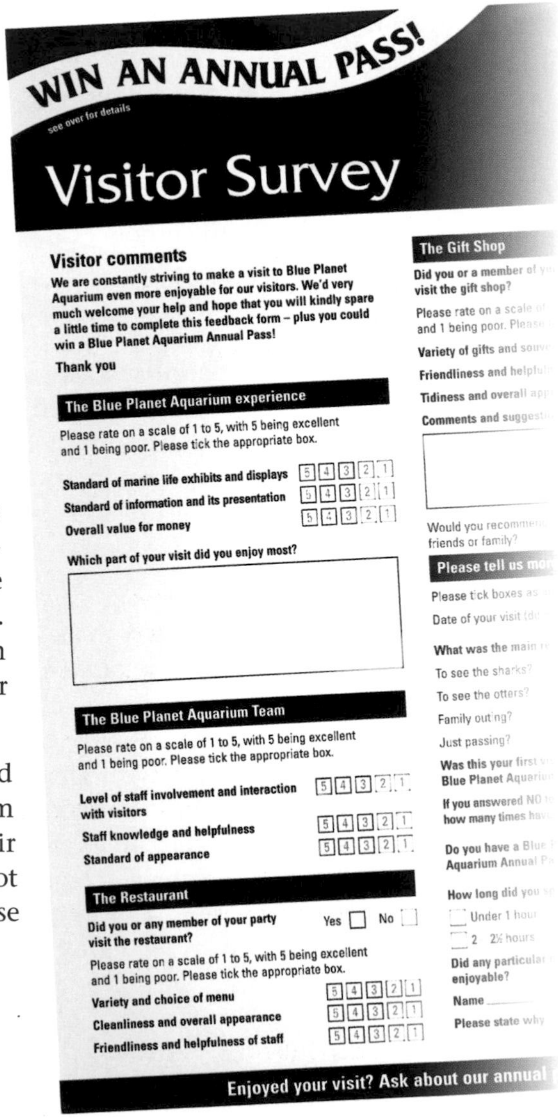

WIN AN ANNUAL PASS!

see over for details

Visitor Survey

Visitor comments

We are constantly striving to make a visit to Blue Planet Aquarium even more enjoyable for our visitors. We'd very much welcome your help and hope that you will kindly spare a little time to complete this feedback form – plus you could win a Blue Planet Aquarium Annual Pass!

Thank you

The Blue Planet Aquarium experience

Please rate on a scale of 1 to 5, with 5 being excellent and 1 being poor. Please tick the appropriate box.

Standard of marine life exhibits and displays	5	4	3	2	1
Standard of information and its presentation	5	4	3	2	1
Overall value for money	5	4	3	2	1

Which part of your visit did you enjoy most?

The Blue Planet Aquarium Team

Please rate on a scale of 1 to 5, with 5 being excellent and 1 being poor. Please tick the appropriate box.

Level of staff involvement and interaction with visitors	5	4	3	2	1
Staff knowledge and helpfulness	5	4	3	2	1
Standard of appearance	5	4	3	2	1

The Restaurant

Did you or any member of your party visit the restaurant? Yes ☐ No ☐

Please rate on a scale of 1 to 5, with 5 being excellent and 1 being poor. Please tick the appropriate box.

Variety and choice of menu	5	4	3	2	1
Cleanliness and overall appearance	5	4	3	2	1
Friendliness and helpfulness of staff	5	4	3	2	1

The Gift Shop

Did you or a member of y[...]
visit the gift shop?

Please rate on a scale [...]
and 1 being poor. Pleas[...]

Variety of gifts and sou[...]

Friendliness and helpfu[...]

Tidiness and overall ap[...]

Comments and sugges[...]

Would you recommen[...]
friends or family?

Please tell us mo[...]

Please tick boxes as [...]

Date of your visit [...]

What was the main [...]

To see the sharks?

To see the otters?

Family outing?

Just passing?

Was this your first [...]
Blue Planet Aquari[...]

If you answered NO [...]
how many times ha[...]

Do you have a Blue [...]
Aquarium Annual P[...]

How long did you [...]

☐ Under 1 hour

☐ 2 – 2½ hours

Did any particular [...]
enjoyable?

Name ______

Please state why

Enjoyed your visit? Ask about our annual [...]

▶ ***Figure 2.5** Part of a customer comment card*

Observation

Watching customers and recording what is seen is a market-research technique. Observations made by leisure and tourism organisations include counting how many customers enter, leave or use particular facilities. Here are some other market-research questions that can be answered by observation:

- How old are the customers?
- What is their gender?
- What size group are they part of?

CaseStudy Flamingoland Theme Park and Zoo

Flamingoland is a visitor attraction consisting of a zoo and a theme park that includes a range of rides from 'white-knuckle' to those suitable for small children. It is in North Yorkshire between Leeds and Scarborough. Leeds is one important source of leisure visitors. Tourist families staying in Scarborough are a second target market. Figure 2.6 shows the location of Flamingoland.

Market-research techniques

There are two types of market-research techniques: primary and secondary. Primary research involves finding data yourself. In this case, it means that Flamingoland pays to have new data found for it. Secondary research means studying data that already exist. Flamingoland obtains some of its market-research data from sources that exist already.

Primary market-research techniques used by Flamingoland include questionnaires that are given out to customers in the theme park and completed either there or later on and posted back. In addition, admission data can be collected electronically. Flamingoland has a range of ticket types:

- adult
- child under 12
- child under 3 (free)
- senior citizen

▲ *Figure 2.6 Location of Flamingoland Theme Park and Zoo*

- wheelchair user (and carer)
- family
- mini-group (12–25 people) — pre-paid
- mini-group — pay on arrival
- larger group (25 or more people) — pre-paid and pay on arrival
- schools and uniformed groups (e.g. scouts and girl guides) — pre-paid and pay on arrival
- season tickets

The existence of such a wide range of ticket types provides a valuable market-research database.

Secondary sources of market-research data available to Flamingoland include:

- Tourist Board data: just as the Low Wood Hotel in Windermere (see pages 80–81) can use information from the Cumbria Tourist Board, Flamingoland is able to call on the services of its regional tourist board — the Yorkshire Tourist Board.
- National databases such as those of the government's Office of National Statistics and the website **www.staruk.org**.
- Information on general market trends reported in the media, including the leisure and tourism trade press.
- The Association of Leading Visitor Attractions provides statistical information that Flamingoland management can use to assess its market performance against other visitor attractions.

Have a Go

Know and understand	Apply what you know	Investigate
1 Explain, using examples, the difference between primary and secondary market-research techniques.	**2** For a visitor attraction other than Flamingoland suggest primary and secondary market-research techniques that its management could use.	**3** Choose one leisure or tourism facility. Design a questionnaire aimed at discovering the market segments that the organisation serves most.

Chapter

2.2

The marketing mix

The marketing mix is one of four main marketing tools that leisure and tourism organisations use:

- target marketing
- market research
- marketing mix
- SWOT analysis

We looked at target marketing and market research in Chapter 2.1. SWOT analysis is the subject of Chapter 2.3.

The marketing mix is a blend of four key ingredients, the 4 Ps:

- **product** (products and services — what a leisure and tourism organisation offers its customers)
- **price** (what the products and services cost customers)
- **promotion** (how organisations encourage people to want their products and services)
- **place** (where the products and services are available)

The marketing mix can be divided into two sections:

- products, services and prices
- promotion and place

Products, services and prices

Table 2.1 gives some examples of products and services that leisure and

▼ **Table 2.1
Examples of leisure
and tourism
products and
services**

Organisation	Products and services
Leisure	
Leisure centre	Swimming session in the pool
Library	Book lending
Video-rental shop	DVD hire
Cinema	Film showings
Pub	Bar meal
Art gallery	Posters for sale
Sports stadium	Rental of hospitality box
Theme park	Family admission
Travel and tourism	
Travel agency	Booking package holidays
Tour operator	Resort representative
Tourist information office	Local sightseeing advice
Online travel booker	Car hire over the internet
Hotel	En-suite rooms
Airline	International air travel

tourism organisations provide for their customers. Each product and service has a price (even if it is free and the price is zero). Leisure and tourism organisations have a pricing policy, which is a set of guidelines used to decide what to charge for products and services.

Products and services

Figure 2.7 shows some well-known leisure and tourism brands. Brand names are used to identify leisure and tourism facilities and organisations. They help the organisations to market products and services.

▼ **Figure 2.7**
Some leisure and tourism brands

They are names that people recognise or find easy to remember. Products and services provided by the organisation are branded (named after the brand). This identifies the products and services with the image and the quality that marketing has given the brand. If people have heard the brand name before and think that it represents good quality and value for money, this can help to sell the product or service.

After-sales service

After buying a leisure and tourism product or service, customers may receive follow-up service from the organisation. Customers of a tour operator may get an evaluation form (Figure 2.4), which gives them the chance to feed back on how their holiday went. The tour operator will post them a copy of next year's brochure and send online updates to customers' e-mail addresses. Such services help satisfy customers so that they are more likely to provide repeat business for the tour operator. They could also pass positive messages about the organisation to other people who may become customers. All this is good marketing for any leisure and tourism organisation.

Outside the leisure and tourism industries, after-sales service is often concerned with the maintenance and repair of consumer products. For example, after a garage has sold a customer a new car, part of the after-sales service may be to provide a free initial service following a specified running-in period. Products such as cars are material objects and are said to be tangible products, because they can be touched or held.

Many leisure and tourism products and services are intangible — they cannot be touched or held. A package holiday is a good example. After-sales service can be provided by the tour operator once customers have returned home (e.g. the evaluation form in Figure 2.4). Services such as those provided by resort representatives, which are available during the holiday, are also after-sales. This is because a tour operator's package-holiday customers pay for their holidays in advance, so the resort-representative service is likely to be provided after the sale is made.

Although a tangible product, such as a television set, can be returned to the shop if it goes wrong, the same cannot be done with an intangible product like a package holiday. Resort representatives deal with issues on the spot (e.g. if a customer is allocated an inadequate hotel room).

Product life cycle

This concept is based on the idea that products are born when they are launched and die when customers no longer want them. In between sales of the product increase at first and then go down. Figure 2.8 shows the four phases of the product life cycle: introduction, growth, maturity and decline.

In the UK, seaside resorts such as Brighton, Blackpool and Scarborough grew in popularity as tourism destinations in the nineteenth century, after the introduction of railways. In the first half of the twentieth century, the resorts expanded as people had more paid holidays than before. This was the mature phase of the product life

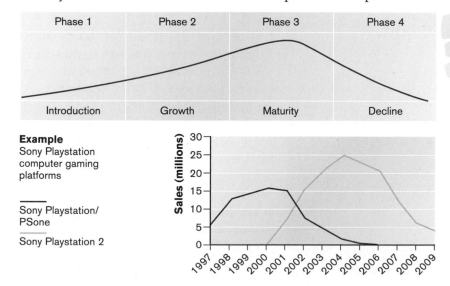

◀ *Figure 2.8
The product life
cycle*

cycle. After the 1950s, the rising popularity of summer holidays in the sun led to decline in the UK resorts. Attractions and hotels located in seaside resorts have undergone the same stages.

Marketing has two roles in the product life cycle:
- to help a product through the early phases of the cycle (introduction, growth and up to maturity)
- to combat the fall of sales in the later part of the product life cycle (from maturity to decline)

▲ **Figure 2.9**
St Nicholas Hotel in Scarborough

► **Figure 2.10**
Spinnaker Tower in Portsmouth

Publishing Pictures

As hotels in seaside resorts suffered declining sales, organisations began to rethink their marketing strategies. They picked on new target markets and offered new products such as:
- business conferences
- group deals for coach operators bringing parties of retired people out of season
- weekend-break deals

The aim of these new products was to slow down and try to reverse the decline phase of the product life cycle. For larger hotels in many UK seaside resorts, such marketing has been successful, as in the case of the St Nicholas Hotel in Scarborough (Figure 2.9).

The Spinnaker Tower in Portsmouth (Figure 2.10) is a twenty-first-century visitor attraction. It is 170 metres high and visitors can ride to the top in either a panoramic lift or a high-speed internal lift for views stretching many kilometres in all directions — over the Isle of Wight and the English Channel, the city of Portsmouth and the inland countryside. Opened in 2005, Spinnaker Tower's marketing aim is to introduce the attraction to a wide audience of potential customers and then to build trade in order to move as quickly as possible through the growth phase of the product life cycle.

Price

The price is the amount of money that leisure and tourism organisations charge for a product or service. The actual selling price is what customers pay. Leisure and tourism organisations consider a number of factors when they decide what the actual selling price will be. Some have pricing policies, which are guidelines that help facility managers set prices. The following factors need to be considered:

- **Cost of providing the product or service**: usually the aim is to charge a price that covers the organisation's costs. When an organisation is charging just enough to pay its bills from suppliers and for overheads such as fuel and heating, it is said to be 'breaking even'. Commercial organisations, such as travel agents and hotels, want to make a profit. A hotel will charge prices for its rooms that keep it profitable as a business.

- **Competition**: other leisure and tourism organisations providing similar products and services at lower prices may attract more customers. A leisure and tourism organisation, such as a health club, should check the prices charged by other health clubs in its area to make sure that its own prices are competitive. Leisure and tourism organisations do not always compete with each other using price alone: quality matters, too. A luxury hotel is able to charge higher room rates than a budget hotel because of the higher quality that it offers.

- **What the market will bear**: this means the highest price that a sufficient number of customers will pay. If a profitable price for a product or service is higher than customers think reasonable, then there is no point offering the product. Often, competition means that leisure and tourism organisations (e.g. a take-away restaurant) do not charge the highest price that the market will bear. Instead they set a lower price that a sufficient number of customers find attractive.

- **Discounts and credit terms**: to increase or maintain their market share, leisure and tourism organisations offer lower prices or discounts on some products and services. Market share is the fraction of the market for a product or service that an organisation or facility captures. The Cadbury World visitor attraction (see the case study below) offers discounts to certain market segments, such as families.

  Credit terms are the agreements that leisure and tourism organisations make with customers who want to delay payment in some way. This can be paying by instalments or using a credit card. Some online ticket agencies charge an extra price (premium) if customers pay using a credit card. Paying by instalment is not common in the leisure and tourism industries. It is more usual in retailing when customers buy expensive goods like washing machines. However, a health club that charges an annual membership fee may allow customers to pay monthly. The agreed credit terms could be that each monthly payment is slightly higher than one twelfth of the annual fee. As a general rule, products and services provided on credit attract a small price premium.

Marketing leisure and tourism products and services includes making customers aware of the benefits of a particular organisation's prices. A cinema wants customers to know that its prices are reasonable and competitive for the quality it provides, as well as informing them about what discounts are available.

CaseStudy Cadbury World

Cadbury World is a visitor attraction in Bournville, Birmingham, run by the Cadbury chocolate-making firm.

Products and services

- A walking tour of the main indoor exhibition on two floors (see Figure 2.11): Table 2.2 shows different elements of the tour that appeal to different age groups, satisfying customers from a range of market segments. This is important for marketing Cadbury World, because satisfied customers will tell other people about their good experience. These people are potential future customers. Those who visit the Cadbury World exhibition and have a good time tell more people, and so on (the multiplier effect).
- The World's Biggest Cadbury Shop selling Cadbury's chocolate and Cadbury World souvenirs. The shop is located at the exit from the main exhibition, by the main entrance and foyer. This is good marketing. It maximises the chance of visitors spending money since they see the shop as they arrive and again as they finish the tour. It is common practice in visitor attractions, museums and galleries to position

gift shops and cafés at key points (e.g. beside main entrances and at the ends of walk-through routes).
- Restaurant meals, snacks, drinks and fast food (which is sold through outlets that are open at busier times).
- An interactive show featuring Cadbury World characters in Cadbury Land, which is separate from the main exhibition area.
- A children's play area in Cadbury Land and the interactive show pitched at families and appealing to younger customers.
- The Cadbury Collection — an exhibit telling the story of Cadbury's that is more likely to appeal to older teenager and adult customers, including retired people.
- Access to the upper exhibition floor for disabled customers via lifts. There is a pushchair parking bay at the foot of one of the lifts. Health and safety fire regulations do not allow pushchair access to the Packaging Plant or the second floor of the exhibition building.
- Toilet facilities, including disabled toilets.
- First-aid post.
- Signage (signs to provide information for customers) including footprints painted on the

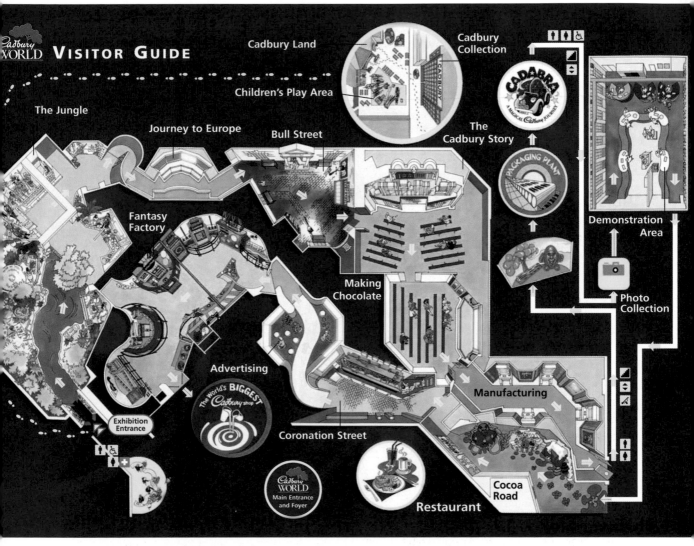

Figure 2.11
The Cadbury World tour

Element of the tour	Market-segment appeal
'The Jungle': the story of chocolate	Families, older children, adults
'Journey to Europe': the arrival of chocolate in Europe	Teenagers, adults
'Bull Street': Cadbury products of the past	Adults, including senior citizens
'Making Chocolate'	Families, adults
'Manufacturing': the industrial process	Adults, students
'Cocoa Road': Cadbury World characters	Younger children, families
'Coronation Street': how the Street was modelled in chocolate	Adults

Table 2.2
Elements of the Cadbury World tour and their market segment appeal

ground to guide visitors from the main exhibition to Cadbury Land and the Cadbury Collection.

- Reception and ticket collection point: Cadbury World visitors are encouraged to book in advance (e.g. via the internet).

Prices

Table 2.3 gives details of 2005 admission prices to Cadbury World. Prices change over time and the latest admission prices can be found on the Cadbury World website. The basic adult price is calculated using the factors outlined earlier in this chapter: profitability, competition, what the market will bear and discounts. Discounts are available for certain categories of customer: children, students, senior citizens and various groups.

Group discounts include those for families and school parties. Lower prices make it more likely that families will think Cadbury World is an affordable

Customer type	Price
Adult	£10.50
Child (4–15)	£7.90
Child (under 4)	Free
Student/senior citizen	£8.30
Family	£32.00 (two children) £38.50 (three children)
School groups: adult child	£8.00 (peak), £7.30 (off-peak) £6.00 (peak), £5.00 (off-peak)
Annual passes	From £20.40 (child) to £93.20 (family with three children)

▲ *Table 2.3 2005 admission prices for Cadbury World*

attraction. Families are likely to spend additional money in the restaurant, at the fast-food outlets and on chocolates and souvenirs in the World's Biggest Cadbury Shop.

Have a Go

Know and understand

1 Draft a letter for Cadbury World to send to schools and colleges explaining its products and services and the prices that Cadbury World can offer them.

Apply what you know

2 Think of a product or service offered by a leisure and tourism organisation that you know.

 a Discuss which phase of the product life cycle it has reached.

 b Explain your decision.

Investigate

3 a Research the range of products and services offered by a leisure and tourism organisation and its pricing structure.

 b Explain why the organisation offers different prices to different customer groups.

Promotion and place

Promotion

Promotional materials and techniques are marketing tools that leisure and tourism organisations use to make people aware of their products, services and prices in ways that encourage custom. Promotional materials are objects — pieces of marketing — whereas techniques are ways of distributing materials to potential customers. Potential customers are people who may become actual customers of leisure and tourism organisations. Table 2.4 gives examples of promotional materials and techniques to show the difference between them.

Advertising is a promotional technique, whereas advertisements are promotional materials. Advertising is the design, positioning and distribution of advertisements. Forms of advertisement include posters, flyers, panels in the printed media (e.g. newspapers and magazines), television and radio commercials and internet pop-ups. Figure 2.12 shows an example of an advertisement.

Technique	Material
Advertising	Advertisements
Direct marketing	Brochures and leaflets
Public relations	Merchandising materials
Personal selling	Videos
Displays	Press releases
Sponsorship	Internet websites
Demonstrations	
Sales promotions	

▲ *Table 2.4 Promotional techniques and materials*

Gala Threatre, Cinema and Kafé Gala

Durham's premier entertainment venue is fully accessible to everyone. With a great range of theatre and cinema shows make sure you don't miss out and join our mailing list to receive your programme of events.

Kafé Gala on the ground floor of the Gala has a relaxing atmosphere in which to enjoy light refreshments before or after a show or just when shopping in the Gala.

Level access to the theatre is at the bottom of Claypath which provides direct access into the ground floor of the Gala complex. inside there are lifts to all floors to enable all users full access.

There are wheelchair spaces in the theatre and cinema auditorium and refreshments can be brought to less able patrons before and during intervals within the showings. An accompanying guest is welcomed free of charge to every show. Guide, hearing and other working dogs are also welcome to all areas of the Gala complex.

Gala has disabled toilet facilities throught out the building.

For more information please contact us and we will be happy to meet your needs.

Gala

Box Office: 0191 332 4041
Group Bookings: 0191 332 4045
Gala Theatre, Millennium Place, Durham, DH1 1WA
www.galadurham.co.uk

▲ *Figure 2.12 An advertisement for Durham Gala Theatre*

In **direct marketing**, a leisure and tourism organisation promotes its products and services directly to the customer, missing out the media in which advertisements usually appear. Promotional material sent through the post to customers on the leisure and tourism organisation's database is called a mailshot. Mailshots are an example of direct marketing, as is 'junk mail'. Figure 2.13 shows an example of direct marketing material.

AFRICAN KITCHEN GALLERY
Runner's Up Time Out Award 2004
102 Drummond Street
Euston London
NW1 2HN
T/F: 020 7383 0918

WE SERVE DELICIOUS
AFRICAN & CARIBBEAN CUISINE

"The venue is tiny but the flavours are big"
Guy Dimond (Time Out Magazine)

Opening Times: 11.45am to 10.30 pm: Monday to Sunday
Eat In or Take Away
Euston, Euston Square, Warren Street Stations

◀ **Figure 2.13** Direct marketing material

▼ **Figure 2.14 Example of a bad public relations news story**

Tourists' Cancun 'hell'

British tourists are claiming they were abandoned by their tour operators when Hurricane Wilma tore through Cancun last weekend. Tens of thousands of tourists were stuck for days in over-crowded shelters with little bedding or food.

Good public relations, i.e. when a leisure and tourism organisation gets favourable reports in the media, is important for the successful marketing of products and resources. Tour operators try to make sure that media stories about them are favourable. A news story about customers becoming stranded abroad because of a hurricane (Figure 2.14) would be a public-relations problem.

Personal selling is when a leisure and tourism organisation markets its products and services through employees who talk directly to potential customers in an effort to persuade them to buy. For example, a tour operator resort representative (see Case Study on pages 72–73) may use a welcome meeting to try to sell extras such as excursions. Figure 1.62 on page 73 shows an excursion sold to tourist customers of a UK outbound tour operator in Mallorca.

Displays are another promotional technique. Hotels often have displays of leisure organisations' leaflets in reception.

Sponsorship of an event or of another leisure and tourism organisation such as a football club may cost money but can be good marketing because the sponsor's logo and name can be seen by many people in a positive light. Figure 2.15 shows an example of McDonald's sponsoring the FA Community Shield in 2004.

Demonstrations of a leisure and tourism product or service in action can be an effective promotional technique as a showcase for potential customers. For example, a local leisure centre or sports club could organise an open day at which demonstrations were given by

members of leisure activity classes. A demonstration of martial arts, for example, could encourage new members to join a karate club.

Sales promotions are temporary **marketing campaigns**. To increase sales of a leisure and tourism product or service, organisations can run limited special offers for new customers. If customers like the product, they may continue to pay for it after the special offer has ended. For example, a health club may offer specially reduced memberships in January when some middle-aged adults make New Year's resolutions to get fit. This promotion could lead them to take out longer-term memberships at the usual rate after the offer has finished.

Leisure and tourism organisations use these techniques to promote their facilities, products and services. The techniques that they choose are those they think are best at promoting a particular product or service to a certain type of customer. For example, it would be appropriate for a village hall (see Chapter 1.1, Figure 1.11) to advertise its youth club using posters and flyers, whereas a large travel agency may opt for television commercials.

Promotional materials
The promotional materials used by leisure and tourism organisations vary widely. A summary of these materials is given in Figure 2.16. A **flyer** differs from a **leaflet** because a flyer is one sheet of unfolded paper whereas a leaflet is folded. Leaflets used by leisure and tourism facilities are often folded twice to create a two-sided, three-panelled piece of promotional material on which a lot of information can be presented. Figures 2.17 and 2.18 are examples of a flyer and a leaflet from the Gala Theatre in the tourist city of Durham.

▲ *Figure 2.15 McDonald's sponsored the FA Community Shield in 2004*

▶ **Figure 2.16**
Summary of promotional materials

Flyers are sometimes distributed by hand or through letterboxes. They are also made available on displays in tourist information centres or in the foyers of hotels and restaurants that cater for tourists and visitor attractions. Unlike posters they are not mounted on noticeboards or stuck to billboards.

▼ **Figure 2.17**
A flyer advertising a Christmas concert

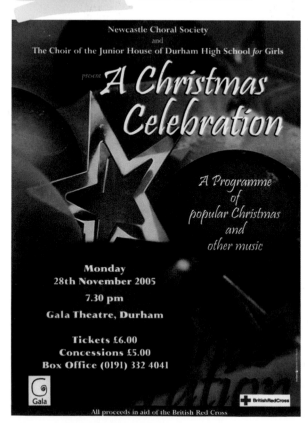

Some leisure and tourism organisations use **merchandising materials** to help their marketing. Figure 2.21 shows a 'freebie' pen given by a hotel, which customers are invited to take away. Contact details of the hotel are printed on it, so the pen becomes an advertisement. The gift shops of many visitor attractions sell souvenirs such as fridge magnets, pencils and mugs that display their logos. These are not just mementos for visitors: they are also promotional materials and act as advertisements that others will see.

Public-relations management is a promotional technique. **Press releases** are promotional materials often produced by public-relations personnel. Generally, a press release is a short written statement that a leisure and tourism organisation thinks is newsworthy. A local leisure centre with a major new facility such as a new sports

▲ **Figure 2.18**
A leaflet for the Gala Theatre cinema

hall may send press releases to local newspapers and radio stations in the hope that news of the opening will be reported or broadcast. This is good marketing for little cost compared to paying for an advertisement.

Videos, CDs and DVDs are used by tour operators and tourist information services to promote tourism. Many visitor attractions produce souvenir videos or sponsor educational CDs.

Websites are virtual promotional materials on the internet. Many destinations and leisure and tourism organisations have their own websites. Examples can be drawn from all sectors of both the leisure and the travel and tourism industries. Exceptions are small, local organisations for which a website may be inappropriate if their market is in a small locality. A local cricket club, for example, may find that a website is unnecessary.

▼ **Figure 2.19**
Village Leisure Hotels 'freebie' pen

How effective promotional materials are depends on:
- how they are designed
- the words and images used
- how widely they are distributed to customers

CaseStudy | Promoting a concert at the Gala Theatre, Durham

The purpose of the flyer (Figure 2.17) is to promote a Christmas concert performed by two choirs at the Gala Theatre. This one-off event takes place on one evening and features amateur singers. A flyer is an appropriate form of promotional material to grab attention and convey necessary information. A leaflet would be more expensive and unnecessary in this case.

Use of colour is appropriate. Orange and red are warm colours that give a seasonal impression, as do the shapes of Christmas stars and baubles. Different fonts and sizes of text are used. They add interesting variety without going over the top. Too many different styles can make a piece of promotional material so busy that its central message is lost. The text is clear in white and arranged on the flyer so that the title 'A Christmas Celebration' and details of time and place are obvious to the viewer. Price, time, location and contact information is useful. Concessions are widely understood to mean children, students and senior citizens. Whether unemployed people would receive a concessionary price is not clear, but too much information would spoil the overall appearance of the flyer. The text 'Christmas Celebration' in red at the bottom is similar in colour to the lowest bauble and therefore is difficult to read.

It is assumed that potential customers know where the Gala Theatre is in Durham. Extra information, such as as a map, would be more appropriate on a leaflet, on which more space is available.

Two logos are used on the flyer. The Gala Theatre logo is good for marketing because customers might recognise it on the theatre's other products and services and be attracted to use them. The British Red Cross logo indicates that a charity benefits from the proceeds of the concert (repeated as text underneath). This could encourage potential customers to spend their money on tickets, particularly at Christmas. Overall, the flyer is effective.

Good leisure and tourism promotional material should grab *attention*, create *interest* in the product or service and build a *desire* for it with information on how to take *action* — AIDA:

- attention
- desire
- interest
- action

The flyer in Figure 2.17 achieves all of these goals. The overall design is eye-catching (attention) and has a Christmas feel to create interest. A charitable destination for profits, raises the desire to help others at Christmas. It is clear that customers can ring to book tickets (action).

Promotional campaigns

Promotional campaigns are carefully structured sequences of marketing effort that run for a specified period of time. For example, a tour operator may plan a campaign to promote summer outbound holidays. National tour operators may use television advertising as a promotional technique. The campaign could open a few days before Christmas to whet the appetites of potential customers. Between Christmas and New Year, continuing into early January, more frequent and longer commercials might be broadcast. These could be backed up by printed advertisements in newspapers and magazines and by updating the tour operator's website. The campaign could end later in January, but other promotional efforts would continue. Such a campaign is a *temporary* promotional push.

Practical scenario **Producing a piece of promotional material**

You can follow the flowchart in Figure 2.20 to produce a piece of promotional material yourself. Types of promotional material that you can design easily are:

- posters
- flyers
- leaflets
- internet pop-up/home pages
- radio advertisements

Leisure and tourism organisations from all the key components may run time-limited promotional campaigns. Such organisations take five factors into consideration when planning campaigns in order to gain most benefit at an appropriate cost:

- **objectives**: what the campaign sets out to achieve
- **target market**: who the campaign is aimed at
- **promotional techniques**: which technique to use
- **promotional materials**: which materials to use
- **evaluation**: how to check on the success of the campaign, for example by studying data such as admission numbers or holiday bookings taken during the campaign to find out whether they have increased and whether the extra number is worth the costs of mounting the campaign

Place

The fourth 'P' of the marketing mix is place. This is where the product or service is accessed by the customer. A take-away restaurant provides its core product (meals) at its premises. It is important for marketing the restaurant that it is situated in a place that is convenient for its customers. Such locations include:

- in a town or village centre
- on a main road leading from a town centre
- in a residential area
- on an out-of-town leisure park

These locations are easily accessed by people who live nearby (residential area) or by people who are passing on foot (town centre) or by car (main road). Leisure parks suit customers who have cars and people who go to the leisure park to visit another leisure facility such as a multiplex cinema.

What are you promoting?
Narrow it down.

Who is the target market?
Be clear in your own mind.

What information will you present?
What does the target need to know?

What format will you use?
Flyer? Leaflet? Poster? Other?

Prepare a draft design.
Use AIDA.

Review your design
Test it out on someone else.

Produce your material
Consider colour carefully.

▲ **Figure 2.20** *Flowchart for producing a piece of promotional material*

Some take-away restaurants offer delivery services. Typically, customers access these services from home by telephone. The restaurant management needs to decide the area within which it is prepared to deliver. It is important for the restaurant's profitability that it delivers far enough to capture customers, but not to such great distances that costs of fuel and driver time are too high.

Conclusion

Leisure and tourism organisations consider all four components of the marketing mix (product, price, promotion and place) not only separately but also blended together. There is a strong combination of price and product in the promotion of the Christmas charity concert in Figure 2.17. The ticket price is one that customers may think reasonable for an amateur show, given that proceeds are for the British Red Cross.

The importance of each 'P' component varies between organisations and from campaign to campaign. For example, the importance of price is raised if an organisation has competitors close to it. The only computer game shop in a town will place less weight on the price ingredient of its marketing mix than would be the case if a competitor started up in business nearby.

Have a Go

Know and understand	Apply what you know	Investigate
1 a Sketch the main elements of the flyer in Figure 2.17. b Annotate your sketch to show the strengths and weaknesses of the flyer.	2 Evaluate a piece of promotional material using AIDA. a Give each feature (A, I, D and A) a mark out of five. b Explain your marks.	3 a Collect a range of promotional materials used by a leisure and tourism organisation. b Find out what promotional techniques the organisation uses for distributing these materials.

SWOT analysis

SWOT analysis is used by leisure and tourism organisations to monitor how well they are doing. They consider their provision of products and services under four headings:

- strengths (S)
- weaknesses (W)
- opportunities (O)
- threats (T)

Strengths and weaknesses refer to internal factors that the organisation can control. Leisure and tourism organisations aim to have more strengths than weaknesses. Strengths are played up in marketing the organisation. Weaknesses are issues that need to be addressed.

Opportunities and threats are the second half of SWOT. They are external because they are outside the control of the organisation. Opportunities and threats come from the environment in which leisure and tourism organisations operate. Opportunities are chances to do well, perhaps by attracting more customers or taking more money. Threats are challenges that need to be overcome if the organisation is to do well. The activities of competitors are often threatening to a commercial leisure and tourism organisation.

CaseStudy SWOT analysis of Buckerell Lodge Hotel in Exeter

Buckerell Lodge Hotel (Figure 2.21) is a 53-bedroom hotel in the suburbs of the city of Exeter. Exeter is in Devon in southwest England. It is a historic city with a famous university and attracts both leisure and business tourists. Buckerell Lodge Hotel is in the suburb

**Figure 2.21
Buckerell Lodge
Hotel in Exeter**

Buckerell Lodge Hotel, Exeter

of Topsham, on Topsham Road, just over 3 km from Exeter's main railway station, Exeter St David's. Figure 2.22 shows the location of the hotel in relation to Exeter city centre and the M5 motorway.

Strengths

- The Buckerell Lodge Hotel's peaceful and landscaped grounds are attractive, with outside tables for guests in the summer (Figure 2.23). This is a strength that the hotel can market to leisure customers who want a relaxing break away from home, to business customers who would like to hold a conference in a pretty and quiet place and to local people who want to organise functions such as wedding receptions. The gardens make a good backdrop for wedding photographs.
- The traditional building of the hotel gives it an individual character. The outside of the building is well maintained and is painted a light colour. It has an elegant, country-house appearance with a veranda. These are again strengths that can be marketed to the customer types mentioned above.
- The hotel has 53 bedrooms, which makes it large enough to allow viable public room facilities such as a bar and restaurant and to accommodate conference delegates and wedding guests. The number of rooms is sufficient to encourage potential customers to think that it may be worth telephoning the hotel to check availability at short notice.
- Rooms are all en suite and each has a television, tea- and coffee-making equipment, a hairdryer and a trouser press. This matches the expectation of the target market groups. Ground-floor rooms were refurbished in 2005, making the hotel more marketable to the customer types outlined earlier. The rooms vary in size, so the hotel can market itself as able to accommodate single people, couples and families with children.

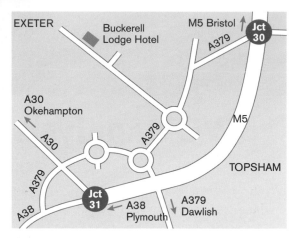

▲ *Figure 2.22 Location of Buckerell Lodge Hotel*

- Five rooms have interconnecting doors between them, allowing larger families to stay in the same room. This flexibility is a marketing advantage for wedding guests.
- There are two wheelchair-accessible rooms, with doors leading onto the gardens. This is an advantage for attracting customers with special access needs.
- The hotel has recently refurbished all public areas and function rooms and has 20 executive rooms available.

▲ *Figure 2.23 Landscaped gardens at Buckerell Lodge Hotel*

- There is a traditional lounge bar called 'Raffles'. It has direct access to the gardens. This appeals strongly to wedding groups and the conference market. Wedding guests and conference delegates can enjoy drinks at the end of the day in pleasant surroundings. Bar meals are served in the bar — a marketing point appreciated by leisure customers who may not always want to eat in the formal setting of the restaurant.
- The restaurant (also called 'Raffles' and shown in Figure 2.24) is wood-panelled and serves local specialities cooked under the supervision of the hotel's own chef. These marketing points appeal to tourists who want to enjoy food from a different region to where they normally live and work.
- Buckerell Lodge has air-conditioned conference facilities — a good marketing point for the business tourist market, especially in summer. Private dining is also offered, catering for groups of between 6 and 80 people. This is attractive for local people who use the hotel as a social facility for events such as birthdays, weddings and anniversaries.
- The hotel is licensed to conduct weddings and so it can market itself as an wedding venue as well as somewhere to hold the reception.
- Buckerell Lodge publishes its own brochure. This full-colour booklet features photographs that promote the other marketing strengths of the hotel. The quality of the brochure as a piece of promotional material is a further strength.
- The hotel is owned and run by the Folio Hotels group. It can afford to invest in the hotel building and facilities and to pay professional staff. The quality of customer service that it can provide is another bonus when it comes to marketing Buckerell Lodge successfully. Folio Hotels features Buckerell Lodge on its company website. The internet is a valuable place

Figure 2.24
The restaurant at Buckerell Lodge Hotel

Buckerell Lodge Hotel, Exeter

to promote a hotel that targets the business market.

Weaknesses

Figure 2.25 shows an extract from notes written by a travel writer. The writer is preparing a review of the Buckerell Lodge Hotel for a forthcoming travel guidebook on Exeter.

▼ *Figure 2.25 Weaknesses of the Buckerell Lodge Hotel*

Not modern

Upper rooms not refurbished in 2005

1 bar and restaurant

Not all wheelchair accessible

Max conference size 80

Not a simple trip from the M5

Not independently owned, nor part of a major brand

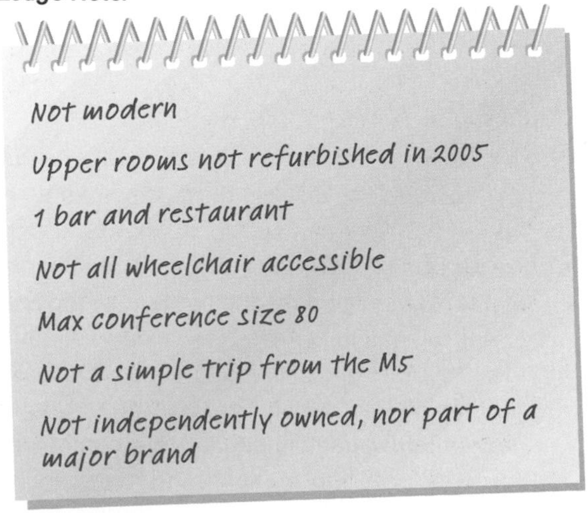

Opportunities and threats

Opportunities and threats are the OT of a SWOT analysis. Table 2.5 lists opportunities for and threats to the Buckerell Lodge Hotel.

Opportunities and threats differ from strengths and weaknesses because they are *external* (outside) factors. They come from the business environment in which the hotel operates. Factors such as the strength of demand for the hotel's products and services and the SWOTs of its competitors combine to create a climate of mixed opportunity and threats that the hotel's marketing must handle. Marketing needs to exploit the opportunities that are presented and try to combat any threats that are posed.

▼ *Table 2.5 Opportunities and threats of the Buckerell Lodge Hotel*

Opportunities	Threats
Exeter City Council tourist information website	Not identified on Exeter City Council tourist information map on website
Dartmoor and Devon's beaches 30 minutes' drive away	No immediate attraction — not on Dartmoor or Devon beaches
1.5 km from central Exeter and accessible from the M5 without having to drive through the city centre	Suburban location, not in walking distance of city centre

Practical scenario — Producing a SWOT analysis

Research

The first step in producing your own SWOT analysis is to find out about the leisure and tourism organisation that you are investigating. Use secondary and primary sources to help you. Secondary sources that may prove valuable are:

- the organisation's own publicity material
- guidebooks to the town and area
- local newspaper articles
- websites, such as those of the local council

A visit to the organisation would be a useful primary source. It could help to be shown around and to record your impressions. An interview with a member of staff, preferably someone with some degree of management responsibility, may provide important information. An advance appointment, made by an adult such as your teacher, is usually appropriate and necessary.

Other potential primary sources are customers of the hotel (past and present) and members of the general public. You could do a survey in the local town centre to assess the impact of the organisation's marketing. Some questions you could try to answer are:

- How many people have heard of the organisation?
- How many would like to visit/use the organisation's facilities?
- How do members of the public regard the organisation in terms of quality and price?

Comparing SWOTs

Comparing the SWOTs of leisure and tourism organisations is useful for assessing the relative merits of organisations that are in competition with each other. Two hotels in the same town compete for the same business. The Holiday Inn Express Hotel in Exeter is a competitor of the Buckerell Lodge Hotel. The hotels are in contrasting buildings and have different target markets. Such pairs of organisations are ideal for comparison by SWOT analysis.

SWOT analysis as a marketing tool

When comparing SWOTs you must first remember that SWOT analysis is a marketing tool. You should look at the marketing implications of each S, W, O and T in turn. What are their similarities? What are their differences? How similar are their strengths (and weaknesses, opportunities and threats) and how significant are their differences?

Have a Go

Know and understand	Apply what you know	Investigate
1 Explain the weaknesses of the Buckerell Lodge Hotel.	**2** Compare the opportunities available to the Buckerell Lodge Hotel with those of another leisure and tourism organisation.	**3 a** Use research to produce a SWOT analysis of a hotel other than Buckerell Lodge. **b** Compare the SWOT analysis of the hotel you have researched with that of Buckerell Lodge.

Building your marketing portfolio

Strand by strand

Build up your coursework for Unit 2 ('Marketing in leisure and tourism') by completing one strand at a time. Make each strand a separate section with its own title, starting every one on a fresh page.

Table 2.6 shows the five strands (A–E) that make up Unit 2. The work for each strand is marked separately and your total score for the unit is found by adding up the marks for the five strands. Each strand is marked according to the quality of your work. The marker decides which of three level descriptors matches your work most closely and gives it a mark in that range. Level 1 describes work of the lowest quality and Level 3 is the highest. Table 2.7 shows the level descriptors for Strand A of Unit 2.

A The pricing of the products and services a leisure and tourism organisation offers

B The promotional techniques and materials the organisation uses (two organisations at Level 3)

C Market-research methods used to identify target markets (two organisations for Levels 1–3)

D A piece of promotional material for your organisation

E SWOT analysis for the organisation (two organisations at Levels 2 and 3)

Your main organisation

You need to choose one main organisation to investigate. This organisation forms the basis of every strand in your Unit 2 coursework. It can come from either leisure or tourism but must clearly belong to one of the key components of the leisure industry or the travel and tourism industry.

▲ Table 2.6
Unit 2 strands

▶ Table 2.7
Level descriptors for
Unit 2, Strand A

Level 1	For the chosen organisation, describe at a basic level the variety of products and services offered and the pricing of the products and services. *(0–3 marks)*
Level 2	For the chosen organisation, produce a clear description of the organisation's products, services and pricing. *(4–7 marks)*
Level 3	For the chosen organisation, analyse relevant information to produce a detailed and accurate account of the organisation's products, services and pricing policy. *(8–10 marks)*

Examples of organisations that you could use are:

- leisure centres
- health clubs
- visitor attractions
- theatres
- museums
- hotels
- coach companies

The size of your main organisation is important. It must be large enough to have marketing materials and strategies that you can research in detail. However, some very large organisations can be difficult to investigate locally because much of their marketing strategy is decided at their national head office.

If you are in any doubt about the suitability of your main organisation you should ask your teacher.

Your second organisation

You must also do some research into the marketing of a second leisure and tourism organisation. This can be any other leisure and tourism organisation, but it is best to pick one that allows you to identify both similarities and differences between the marketing of the two. For this reason, it may be a good idea to choose organisations from the same key component that differ in their approach. In Chapter 2.3, two contrasting hotels in the same city were suggested for comparison by SWOT analysis. This is a good illustration of a suitable pairing of organisations for the whole of Unit 2.

Your second leisure and tourism organisation can be used to make comparisons in three of the five strands (B, C and E). Studying the products, services and prices of the second organisation will also help you in your work for Strand A (see below) if you are aiming for Level 3 marks. The second organisation is needed for the level descriptors highlighted in Figure 2.26.

You need to be clear about which is your main organisation and which is your second choice. You may not swap them round for later strands. Your work for Strand D must be based on the main organisation.

You can complete the strands in any order that your teacher agrees, but it is better for assessment to arrange them in the order in which they appear below. Do not waste time and effort on long, generalised introductions. They will not gain you marks. Get straight on with writing about the products, services and prices of your main organisation.

▶ **Figure 2.26**
When two organisations are needed

Strand	Level 1	Level 2	Level 3
A			
B			███████
C	███████	███████	███████
D			
E		███████	███████

███ Cover two organisations

Strand A

Chapter 2.2, which is about the marketing mix, covers background detail on leisure and tourism products and services, as well as pricing. You should know and understand this chapter's content before you attempt your own coursework for this strand.

Products and services

What are the products and services of your main organisation? You should try to find out all of them. It may help you to visit the organisation when doing this research. Do not worry about which is a product and which is a service. Sometimes it is difficult to separate them completely and you do not have to. Just make sure that you cover both. Describe the products and services — do not just list them or use bullet points. Write in sentences and use brand names when appropriate.

Pricing

What does your main organisation charge for its different products and services? Find out and write a description of them. Do not just copy or cut and paste the price list — you must also describe what the list shows. Avoid handing in work that is simply a list of bullet points.

Consider why different prices are charged:
- for different customer types
- for different products and services
- at different times

You could also ask a manager of the organisation about its pricing policy. Think about the policy yourself and discuss it with fellow students and with your teacher. Incorporate your findings and thoughts in your report.

For Level 3 marks, you need to analyse the information you have collected. You should explain why certain products and services are provided and give reasons for the organisation's pricing structure. You also need to look for links between these two factors. For example, a product or service may be priced cheaply because it is in the early stage of the product life cycle (i.e. an initially low price may stimulate demand). The product life cycle is an appropriate analytical tool for this study. At which stages are your organisation's products and services? Are there links to pricing? At Level 3, you must ensure that your final account is detailed.

Strand B

Find out the range of promotional techniques and materials used by your main organisation. Make sure you that cover both promotional techniques and materials. Do not simply list them — describe them in sentences. Ensure that you write about each one and that what you write is clear. Discuss the breadth of the ranges used — is it a wide range? Which is wider? By how much? Include examples of promotional materials used by the organisation. You must annotate them to show that you understand why they are designed as they are, and you should describe them in words.

Think about what other promotional techniques your organisation could use and include any suggestions in your work. Local organisations may not be able to afford national advertising rates and so television advertising may be another technique you could mention. However, it would be better to think of other techniques and materials that your main organisation could reasonably be expected to use. Use the information on promotion in Chapter 2.2 to give you some ideas (pages 94–101). It will also be helpful if you have studied the promotional techniques and marketing of a second leisure and tourism organisation yourself.

You have to bring your second organisation into your Strand B work if you are to score marks at Level 3. Evaluating the ranges of promotional techniques and products of both your organisations means not just describing the ranges but assessing how appropriate they are to the organisation and drawing a conclusion. You may find it useful to compare the two ranges by looking first at techniques and then at materials and considering each item used.

You can gather much of the information you need by observation and by studying the promotional materials produced by your organisations. However, a visit to one or both of the organisations may provide valuable information that could help improve your final mark.

Strand C

Chapter 2.1 deals with target markets and market research. Your learning in this chapter should help you with Strand C of your Unit 2 coursework. For this strand you have to use both of your organisations to gain marks at all three levels. Even for Level 1, you must look at both organisations if you are to score more than 1 mark.

You need to identify and describe the target markets and the market-research techniques used by both your chosen organisations. As with Strands A and B, you must not just list them or produce a simple series of bullet points. You need to describe in full sentences both target markets and market-research techniques for the two organisations. Then compare them: deal with similarities and differences in turn. First-hand information from a visit to the organisations would be valuable.

Strand D

For Strand D you must produce a piece of promotional material for your *main* organisation — not the second one. Marks are scored for:
- how imaginative your design is
- how appropriate it is for your target audience
- being practical and realistic

There is no need to stray beyond the range of promotional materials commonly used by leisure and tourism organisations. Posters, flyers and leaflets are acceptable. The twice-folded, double-sided, three-panelled leaflet (Chapter 2.2, Figure 2.18) is a standard type used by many leisure and tourism organisations because it is practical and appropriate for the information that needs to be publicised. It may be realistic to produce such a leaflet for your coursework.

Make your design original. Do not follow an already published piece of promotional material so closely that you risk the examiner wondering if it is all your own work. Ensure that all the information that the target audience needs is on your piece of promotional material.

To gain marks at Level 3 you need to show that you have thoughtfully targeted the intended audience. A piece of promotional material can achieve this goal entirely by itself. However, it is advisable to annotate a copy of your promotional material to point out how your work targets the audience. Another approach is to write a commentary to explain the design decisions that you made in producing the promotional material. There is no need to do both unless the commentary contains new information that cannot be gleaned from the material alone.

Strand E

For marks at Level 2 or Level 3, you must carry out SWOT analyses of both your organisations. Begin with your main organisation. Identify its strengths, weaknesses, opportunities and threats. You can do this by considering its promotional materials, by visiting the organisation, by interviewing a manager and by discussion with other students and your teacher.

In writing up the analysis for your main organisation, make sure that you describe each point in some detail. Do not just produce lists of Ss, Ws, Os and Ts. You can begin each S, W, O and T with a bullet point, but several lines of description in sentences should follow. Chapter 2.3 offers an approach to help you with this analysis.

In your descriptions you should not lose sight of the fact that SWOT analysis is a marketing tool. Make sure that you write about strengths, weaknesses, opportunities and threats in terms of how they influence *marketing*. In general:

- Strengths are emphasised by marketing.
- Weaknesses are played down in promotion but are addressed by adjusting the other 3Ps of the marketing mix (product, place and price).
- Opportunities are targeted by marketing.
- Threats, including competition, are what marketing seeks to counteract.

When you have completed the detailed SWOT analysis for your main organisation, repeat it for your second leisure and tourism organisation. Think about how you did the first one and learn from that to try to improve the second analysis.

Once you are satisfied that you have a detailed SWOT analysis for each organisation, compare them. Consider each strength, weakness, opportunity and threat in turn. Comment on their similarities and differences. For top marks, try to go beyond simply identifying the similarities and differences of the Ss, Ws, Os and Ts. Describe the extent of the differences and offer some thoughts on why they are similar or different. Come to a conclusion about which of the strengths, weaknesses, opportunities or threats are most similar and most different.

Presenting your portfolio

Your Unit 2 coursework should be put together in a slim, soft-backed file or folder. Do not use a bulky ring binder or put each page in a separate plastic wallet.

Your Unit 2 work is entirely separate from that for Unit 3 and should be in a different file. Make sure that each strand is separate and has its own clear title. Present your work as an A4 document. If you have some larger sheets fold them, but make sure that the reader can open them out easily. Do not assemble large appendices of promotional materials. If you need to refer to already published material in your work, then it should be included in the main document and be annotated or commented on there.

Information about building your portfolio for Unit 3 ('Customer service in leisure and tourism') is given in Chapter 3.4.

Topic 3

Customer service in leisure and tourism

Customers

Customers are the people who use the products and services of leisure and tourism organisations. Sometimes they pay money for these products and services, such as buying a holiday or a film ticket. However, some products and services are provided free of charge. For example, customers of a public library can borrow books without paying, and tourist information offices serve non-paying customers. Commercial organisations in the leisure and tourism industries aim to make profits and charge prices accordingly. But such companies may also provide some free products or services in order to help satisfy their customers. For example, a travel agent does not charge customers for advice or brochures, even if they do not book a holiday.

What is customer service?

Customer service is dealing with people who want the products and services that a leisure and tourism organisation provides. Customer service can be:
- face to face
- by telephone
- by e-mail
- by letter
- indirect (e.g. signage — providing signs to guide a customer)

The sketches in Figure 3.1 illustrate these different types of customer service. Table 3.1 gives examples of each in practice.

Good customer service

Good customer service in leisure and tourism keeps customers happy. It makes them feel as though they have been treated politely and in a friendly way, so that they will come back and also tell their friends. Commercial leisure and tourism organisations, such as hotels and

Figure 3.1
Different types
of customer
service

Table 3.1
Examples of
customer
service

visitor attractions, need to provide good customer service because it is beneficial for the organisation: it means people may return to spend more money. New customers might come to spend their money, because they have heard how pleasant and efficient the members of staff are. Figure 3.2 shows an example of good customer service at a hotel reception desk.

Situation	Example
Face to face	Leisure-centre reception employees sell swimming-pool tickets to customers
Telephone	A librarian rings a reader to tell her that the book she ordered is ready for collection
E-mail	An art gallery sends details of its new exhibition to customers on its e-mailing list
Letter	A train company responds to a passenger who has written a letter of complaint about a rude member of staff
Signage	Signs in a hotel lobby show customers where the reception desk is

Figure 3.2 Examples of good customer service scenarios at a hotel reception desk

117

Non-commercial leisure and tourism organisations, such as public libraries and tourist information offices, are public services. Managers of such facilities train staff to provide good customer service and recruit people who enjoy helping customers. A good children's librarian will love books and be keen to pass that enthusiasm on to young people by giving them, their parents and teachers good customer service. This could involve helping them to choose suitable books, reading with them, helping them use their library ticket, providing attractive displays and leading group events based around reading. Doing these tasks in a cheerful and caring way would be good customer service. Leisure and tourism managers want good customer service to be the goal of all their staff. Some people have obvious front-line customer-service roles, such as the hotel receptionist in Figure 3.2. Other members of staff may not deal with customers as part of their main duties. For example, the housekeeping staff in a hotel, who clean and prepare rooms for guests, have less direct customer contact. However, hotel managers still expect them to help customers out whenever they can — for example, by answering any questions that guests may have politely, helpfully and in a friendly way.

Good customer service can be developed by encouraging leisure and tourism employees to ask themselves how they would want to be served if they were the customers. In Figure 3.2, the hotel receptionist imagined what he would want to know if he checked in to a hotel in a city he had not visited before and helped the customer accordingly.

Importance of customer service

Leisure and tourism organisations must ensure that their customers are happy because the customers play the most important part in the organisations' success. Good customer service is vital if people are going to keep paying for an organisation's products and services. Leisure and tourism organisations often try to serve customers better than their competitors and better than their customers expect. Customers who enjoy themselves will come back again. They may also recommend the organisation to other people who could come and spend their money (the multiplier effect). Recommendations are like free advertisements, whether the organisation belongs to the leisure industry (e.g. a health club) or to the travel and tourism industry (e.g. an airline). They bring new business and therefore new money without the organisation having to pay any additional marketing costs. This adds to profits. Good customer service is important because it means more business and more profits for the organisation.

The effects of poor customer service are equally important. Dissatisfied customers may not come back to spend more money. They could also put other people off the organisation. Losing customers through bad customer service is damaging for the organisation's profits. Takings can go down quickly if an organisation gets a bad reputation, so it is important to avoid customer unhappiness. When customers are not satisfied — something that does happen in all leisure and tourism organisations sometimes — managers want to know. They want to deal with the problem and try to sort it out so that customers feel that they have been treated fairly. In Figure 3.3, a restaurant manager explains why this could rescue future business.

▼ *Figure 3.3*
Why dissatisfied customers matter

Maybe it sounds silly, but the restaurant needs dissatisfied customers. Well, we need to know if they are dissatisfied and why.

We need a chance to put things right. We want them to come back and spend more money on our food. We want them to tell their friends and people they work with to come.

If they're dissatisfied, they won't do that. In fact, it'll be worse. They'll put people off coming and that will damage our reputation and trade. That could be fatal for the business. Restaurants need good 'word of mouth' marketing.

So you see I'm happy when people tell me that something isn't right. I'd much rather know. Nothing's ever perfect and we need to know what isn't.

Leisure and tourism organisations monitor carefully the levels of customer satisfaction by a variety of techniques including customer comment surveys (Figure 3.4). If there is customer dissatisfaction, it is important that the causes are known to the manager before news of it spreads among potential customers.

Leisure and tourism facility managers should check whether good customer service is actually being provided. They can observe staff serving customers, but, of course, everyone wants to do well when their boss is watching. Managers need to know how good customer service is when they are not watching and to do this they must ask the customers. Figure 3.4 is a customer survey form available in every hotel room in Village Hotels and Leisure Clubs. On the front of the card the Village Hotels and Leisure Clubs national operations director explains why this guest-survey information matters.

▲ **Figure 3.4
Village Hotels and
Leisure Clubs
customer survey
card**

Because customer service is so important to their success, leisure and tourism organisations train staff in providing it well. In-house customer-service training programmes are organised by larger leisure and tourism organisations. The Novotel hotel group is one example. Younger leisure and tourism employees have the opportunity to receive customer-service training at college, working towards qualifications such as NVQs (National Vocational Qualifications). This is good professional development for staff. Employers are happy to pay for training because the good customer service they expect in return will generate more trade and more money.

Customer-service situations

Customer service is provided in all sorts of different situations, including those that involve:

■ giving people information
■ advising customers

- taking messages and passing them on
- selling and issuing tickets
- record keeping
- sorting out problems
- dealing with dissatisfied customers
- offering extras

Not all of these situations arise every time. Figure 3.5 shows customer-service situations that were encountered by a Transpennine Express train manager on a journey from Liverpool to York.

Customer types

Leisure and tourism organisations have different types of customer. A variety of people can use the same leisure and tourism facility. For example, at a multiplex cinema, different films are shown to appeal to the various market segments. U-certificate films are provided for a family audience that includes young children. Action films are for older customers and other films are just for adults. At certain times, such as during a weekday, there may be special discounts for senior citizens and students in addition to any existing concessions.

Each type of customer should receive good customer service. Staff must recognise customers' needs and then ensure that they are met. Customer types include:

▲ *Figure 3.5*
Customer-service situations on a Transpennine Express train

- individual customers who are on their own or are one of a couple
- groups ranging from families and small numbers of friends to large coach parties
- customers from different age ranges
- people from different cultures
- non-English speakers, or people whose knowledge of English is limited
- business tourists
- people with specific needs

In a sense every customer of a leisure and tourism organisation has specific or special needs. However, what is meant by 'specific needs' here are customers who have:

- limited sight or hearing difficulties
- restricted mobility, such as needing to use a wheelchair
- young children

Leisure and tourism employees are trained to work out and deal with the needs of all the different customer types they are likely to serve in the facility where they work.

Some leisure and tourism facilities have customers that are organisations. For instance, a large visitor attraction such as a theme park may have coach operators as its customers. Airlines pay landing charges to airports and are their customers. Figure 3.6 shows an outlet of catering

*▶ Figure 3.6
The Caffè Ritazza
in Euston Station,
London, is a customer
of Network Rail*

organisation Caffè Ritazza in Euston Station, London. Caffè Ritazza is a customer of Network Rail. Other such customers, which have outlets in stations managed by Network Rail, include UpperCrust, McDonald's, Costa, Millie's Cookies and Delice de France.

Have a Go

Know and understand	Apply what you know	Investigate
1 Explain why good customer service is important to leisure and tourism organisations.	**2** For a leisure and tourism organisation you know about, design a leaflet to show how it meets the requirements of customers with special needs.	**3** Identify by investigation the customer types catered for by any named leisure and tourism organisation.

External and internal customers

Leisure and tourism organisations provide customer service to external and internal customers.

External customers

External customers come from outside the organisation. They are its consumers, visitors or paying guests. Customers often pay for the leisure and tourism products or services that they receive. They should experience good customer service. In commercial organisations it is customers' money that keeps the leisure and tourism business profitable and its staff in jobs. This means that external customers are the most important part of a leisure and tourism facility's work. Good customer service will encourage external customers to return and to tell other people how well they were treated, which should lead to increased numbers of customers and bigger profits.

Internal customers

Internal customers are people inside a leisure and tourism organisation. They are members of its staff. Colleagues provide internal customers with products and services. This happens as part of the organisation's normal operation. People who work in the leisure and tourism industry spend a lot of their time working as part of a team. They look after each other's needs as well as those of external customers. For example, a member of staff who is restocking the shelves in a DVD/video-rental shop should help a busy colleague on the till by opening a second till if there is a queue at the first. Helping a colleague is acting as an internal customer. The needs of external customers in the queue are prioritised over those of the staff member who has to complete the task of restocking shelves. This is good customer service. It is important that employees do not feel above helping out. If a junior colleague is struggling at the till, the manager should be prepared come and help out.

In a larger leisure and tourism facility such as a hotel, there are different departments, including front of house (and reception) and maintenance. Figure 3.7 shows a maintenance card available to guests at the Village Hotel in Coventry. If a guest (an external customer) has a problem, then a customer-service situation like that shown in Figure 3.8 can arise. In this case, the receptionist is an internal customer of the hotel's maintenance department. It is just as important in this situation as in any other that good customer service is given. If the maintenance job is done quickly and efficiently the receptionist will have satisfied the external customer — the person who matters most.

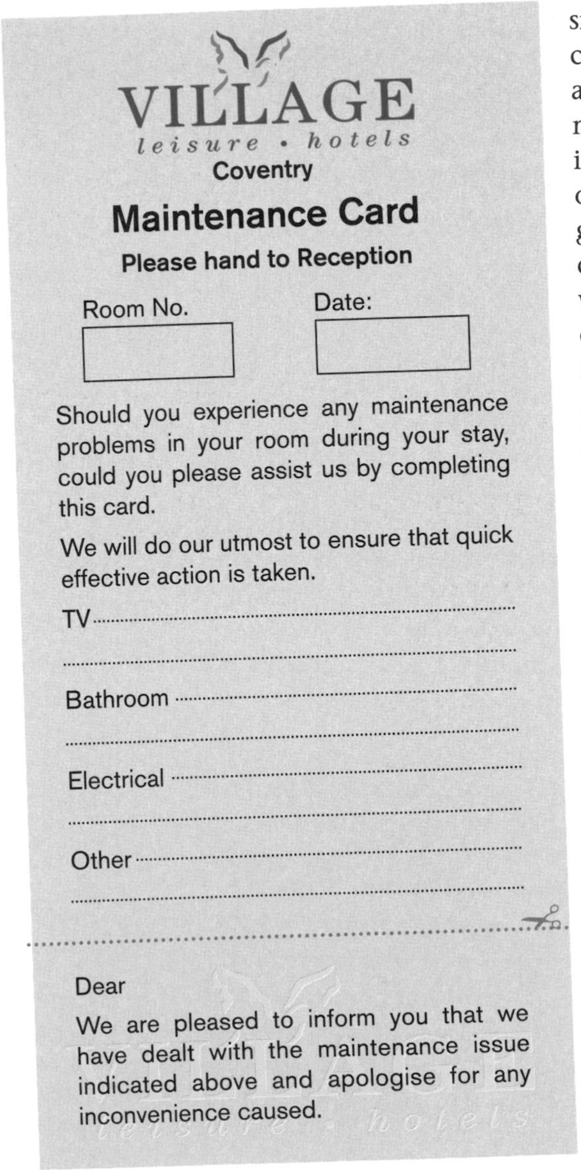

Leisure and tourism organisations train their staff members to have a professional attitude towards each other. In the example in Figure 3.8, it is important that the hotel receptionist feels he can call the maintenance department and can be confident of a professional approach. The maintenance worker should listen courteously, note carefully the request and carry out the job speedily and efficiently. It would also be good internal customer service for the maintenance department to inform reception when the task has been completed.

VILLAGE
leisure • hotels
Coventry
Maintenance Card
Please hand to Reception

Room No.   Date:

Should you experience any maintenance problems in your room during your stay, could you please assist us by completing this card.

We will do our utmost to ensure that quick effective action is taken.

TV ....

Bathroom ....

Electrical ....

Other ....

Dear

We are pleased to inform you that we have dealt with the maintenance issue indicated above and apologise for any inconvenience caused.

◀ *Figure 3.7 Maintenance card from a hotel*

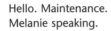

Hello. Maintenance. Melanie speaking.

OK, Peter. I bet it's the remote. I'll take a spare up to the room and see if that sorts it. I'll be about quarter of an hour finishing this job first. I'll ring you and let you know when I'm done.

▼ **Figure 3.8**
An internal customer-service situation

Thanks, Melanie. I'll tell the guest you'll be there in 20 minutes.

Hi Melanie. It's Peter from reception here. The television in Room 415 won't turn on. The customer wants it fixed quickly.

Have a Go

Know and understand	Apply what you know	Investigate
1 Explain the difference between internal and external customers.	**2** A travel agency is producing a training manual for new staff in customer service. You are asked to draw some sketches to show good practice in: **a** external customer service **b** internal customer service	**3** Visit a leisure and tourism facility. List examples of internal and external customer service that you see there.

Dealing with customers

Benefits of good customer service

Good customer service has benefits for leisure and tourism organisations. Sales are likely to go up as satisfied customers come back and recommend the organisation to other people. More customers through repeat business and recommendations mean increased income for commercial leisure and tourism organisations. Their public image is improved, which helps them gain an advantage over their competitors. People are more likely to give their business to an organisation that they have heard provides welcoming, friendly, good-quality customer service.

Benefits also come from staff providing good customer service to each other. As explained in Chapter 3.1, colleagues are internal customers.

▼ *Figure 3.9*
A Pret A Manger
take-away café

Publishing Pictures

Good internal customer service benefits members of staff, as the organisation becomes a better and happier place to work. As a result, employees work more efficiently and achieve greater job satisfaction. Larger leisure and tourism organisations can have a number of branch facilities. For example, the Pret A Manger café chain (from the leisure industry's catering key component) has branches all over the UK (Figure 3.9). The manager of the branch at Newcastle upon Tyne uses the customer-feedback card shown in Figure 3.10 to check the quality of customer service. The front of the card shows that the manager and

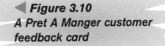

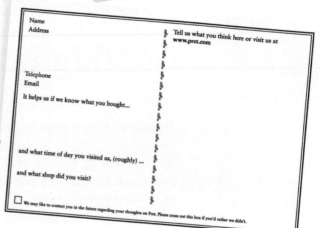

Figure 3.10
A Pret A Manger customer feedback card

his team work closely together to maintain quality customer service.

If staff work together professionally and achieve high standards of customer service in the branch, they receive personal recognition, cash bonuses and have better promotion prospects within the whole organisation. Pret A Manger had 136 take-away cafés in the UK in 2005. The general manager of one of the largest outlets began as an ordinary member of the staff team in one of the first cafés. The UK commercial director (like 60% of Pret A Manger managers) began his career in the same way.

The benefits of good customer service to staff are that they work better and satisfy not only each other (internal customers) but also the vitally important external customers. This leads to more business and higher profits for the organisation.

Communicating with customers

Most jobs in the leisure and tourism industries involve some contact with customers — face to face, by telephone, by e-mail or in writing. Good customer service should be provided in all situations.

Some leisure and tourism jobs involve dealing with customers over the telephone. Phone conversations can take place with the full range of customer types served by the organisation. Employees who communicate with customers by telephone are trained to use appropriate language and to address customers confidently but in a friendly and helpful tone of voice. They know when to pause and allow brief periods of silence to give the customer a chance to think and to respond to what they have heard.

Face-to-face communication

Body language is an important part of providing good customer service in a face-to-face situation. Customers are put at ease by members of staff whose body language suggests that they are alert, interested and listening carefully to what customers are saying. Appropriate body language tends to follow when the member of staff is alert, calm and relaxed (well trained so they know what they are doing) and is genuinely friendly and interested in people. These last two are personal qualities that leisure and tourism employers look for when they are recruiting new members of staff.

One of the most important factors in any other customer service is accuracy. Accurate information given to customers and accurate message taking are essential ingredients. Although customer-service staff, such as resort representatives, may be friendly and cheerful, they can help customers only if they can give information correctly, such as directions to a downtown resort restaurant. Of course, it is impossible to know everything. Figure 3.11 illustrates how one conference manager reacted when she did not know the answer to a customer's question. This is good customer service. The customer received friendly treatment and an accurate piece of information. This example demonstrates how any leisure and tourism job can involve some customer service.

▼ *Figure 3.11
How to give good
customer service
even if you don't
have all the
answers*

Taking messages and listening

Taking accurate messages is a common feature of internal customer service. Telephone messages can come into the office of a leisure and tourism facility all day. At the beginning of the working day a member of the office staff in a leisure centre may need to listen to and record a number of answerphone messages. It is important that these records are accurate. Figure 3.12 illustrates what can happen if mistakes are made. Chapter 3.3 deals with customer records.

Careful listening to what customers say is important for good customer service because it is part of being both polite and accurate. Customers will not be satisfied if they feel that a member of staff has not listened properly. A hotel receptionist who chats to a colleague while also dealing with a customer is not giving good customer service. The customer will think it is rude. The receptionist may misunderstand by not listening properly and give inaccurate or incomplete information as a result.

Inaccurate	Accurate
REDSIDE LEISURE CENTRE MESSAGE	REDSIDE LEISURE CENTRE MESSAGE
Basketball game off	*from Will Elliot* *Medics Basketball Team* *match with Rotary team* *tomorrow at 6.30 cancelled.* *Sports Hall booking therefore* *cancelled too.* *NB. Contact reserve customer*

◀ *Figure 3.12 Inaccurate and accurate message taking*

Open and closed questions

Listening is not always enough by itself. To find out what customers need, appropriate questions need to be asked. There are two types of question:

- open
- closed

Closed questions have short answers, typically 'yes' or 'no'. 'Do you...?' and 'Have you...?' are two ways of beginning closed questions. Open questions allow customers to give a longer answer. The questions are phrased so that customers can shape their replies.

▶ **Figure 3.13 Open and closed questions**

Open

When would you like to go?

Which hotels have caught your eye?

Closed

Are you interested in Ibiza?

Do you know where you would like to stay?

Shall I check the availability on that for you?

▼ **Figure 3.14 Uniforms distinguish staff from customers**

These questions could start with: 'What kind of hotel are you looking for...?' or 'What do you enjoy about the seaside...?'. Figure 3.13 shows a range of open and closed questions asked by a travel consultant. Travel consultants work in travel agents and advise customers about travel and holiday choices.

Jamie Collis/Bannatyne's

Personal presentation

Customers arriving at any leisure and tourism facility form a first impression of what they see. The appearance of the facility itself, its design, décor and tidiness are part of this, as is the appearance of staff. This is important in both the leisure and the tourism industries, as they depend heavily on interaction between people. Staff should be smart, well groomed and easily recognisable. It can be confusing for customers if they cannot distinguish easily between staff and other customers. For this reason, uniforms are common in the leisure and tourism industries. Travel-agency employees often wear uniforms. Figure 3.14 shows a uniformed member of the customer-service staff in a health club. The formality of uniforms varies. In the health club, the informal style suits the relaxed image of the club. Different colours can denote different kinds of staff. Fitness instructors at a health club, for example, may wear different coloured shirts from reception and café-bar staff.

Aspects of personal presentation that matter are:

- dress
- personal hygiene
- personality
- attitude
- behaviour

Customer-service employees who are doing a good job in a leisure and tourism facility should be smartly and correctly dressed, well groomed and be cheerful, friendly and confident. They should display a positive attitude and behave professionally and in an appropriately restrained manner.

These points are important because they matter to customers. Satisfied customers are likely to use the facility again and to spend money. They are likely to return, bringing repeat business, and also to tell other people who will become new customers (the multiplier effect).

Written communication

Writing letters and e-mails is part of customer service. Politeness, attention to what customers need and have said or written, presentation and accuracy are all important. A letter written in response to a customer complaint needs careful consideration of these questions:

- What exactly is the customer's point?
- Is it a fair point?
- Does it need further investigation?
- Have other customers made the same complaint?
- What is an appropriate response?

The reply letter should be accurate in its use of English and give correct information. It needs to be printed on the official company letter- head and be neat and polite but definite in tone. It should be clear who has written the letter and how customers can proceed if they are still unhappy. Handling customer complaints is the subject of Chapter 3.3.

The customer is not always right. The complaint may not be justified or fair to an individual staff member. The letter might need to point this out tactfully using careful phrasing. Figures 3.15 and 3.16 show an annotated letter of complaint from a customer and extracts from a well-phrased reply respectively.

▶ **Figure 3.15**
A letter of complaint

Prime time for families with children

Complaints are not always justified. Is this true? Were they badly behaved?

Dear Sir or Madam

I write to complain about the experience my husband and I had in your restaurant on Friday evening.

We had booked a table in advance for 6.30 p.m. Shortly after taking our seats, a large party of screaming children were given the adjacent table. Their noisy behaviour spoiled the quiet meal we had looked forward to.

We do not intend to waste our money on patronising such a rowdy venue again.

Yours faithfully

Mrs J. Stockton

This is a family restaurant.

Leisure and tourism organisations do not like to lose customers, nor to have other potential customers put off. A small gesture to sweeten the dissatisfied customer may be considered.

▶ **Figure 3.16**
Responding to a complaint

Dear Mrs Stockton

I am sorry that your visit to our family restaurant disappointed you.

We are a family restaurant, and we do welcome children's parties.

Our employees do try to seat couples separately from larger parties. Unfortunately, at busy times, this is not always possible.

I do hope you will be our guests again and I enclose vouchers for you and your husband to enjoy a glass of wine each, with our compliments, when you purchase your next meal from us.

Yours sincerely,

Have a Go

Know and understand	Apply what you know	Investigate
1 Describe **three** different ways in which leisure and tourism staff deal with customers.	**2** Explain why personal presentation is important for travel-agency staff.	**3** Find out how one leisure and one travel and tourism organisation monitor customers' views about the service they receive.

Practical scenario Delivering customer service

As a student of GCSE Leisure and Tourism, you need to practise delivering customer service. You can do this in real leisure and tourism workplaces or in role plays.

Workplace practice

You may be lucky enough to have either a part-time job or a work-experience placement in a leisure and tourism organisation where you serve customers. Chapter 3.4 helps you to build your Unit 3 portfolio. It gives advice on how you can use real customer service in leisure and tourism organisations as part of the coursework for your GCSE.

If your role does not involve customer service, you may be able to watch others dealing with customers. You can learn from this and use your observations in role play.

It may be that you have a job or work experience in a shop. Chapter 3.4 explains why you cannot use this experience, as it stands, in your portfolio. However, you can learn from it and use it as practice and experience in building your customer-service skills. You can role-play leisure and tourism customer service later and do much better. This is because of what are known as transferable skills: skills gained in a non-leisure and tourism workplace can be transferred to a leisure and tourism situation.

Role play

Role play counts the same as real workplace observations when it comes to coursework marks. It is a valuable method of practising customer delivery, too. Face-to-face role plays allow you to practise oral communication skills. However, the playing of roles need not be restricted to face-to-face customer service or to other oral situations like telephone calls. Writing letters and e-mails is just as useful. Taking down the details of a longer answerphone message is a valuable way to develop careful listening.

The two customer-service scenarios described below can be adapted for different:

- customer types
- customer-service situations
- organisations from other key components

Scenarios involving handling customer complaints are considered separately in Chapter 3.3.

Customer-service scenarios

Figure 3.17 illustrates part of a telephone conversation between a customer and a hotel receptionist. The customer is booking a room at the hotel. The customer service provided is good. A clear strength is that the receptionist sells (books) the room and takes contact details. The receptionist has identified the sort of room that suits the

▼ Figure 3.17 Customer service by telephone

Hello. I know it's short notice, but do you have a room for tonight?

Let me just check, sir. Smoking or non-smoking?

Non-smoking, if you have one.

Yes, we do. It is a non-smoking en-suite room with twin beds. It will be £75.00.

Ok. I'll go for that.

That's fine, sir. If you could just give me your name and a contact telephone number. We can sort everything else out when you arrive.

Will you be taking breakfast? That's £4.50 for continental breakfast and £6.95 for full English?

customer's needs. The customer is satisfied and the hotel is making money. Figure 3.18 shows the text of an e-mail exchange between the operator of a secure airport car park and a customer.

Customer service can also involve writing letters. In Figure 3.19 a tour operator is replying to a customer who has asked for written confirmation of a booking made on the telephone.

Enquiry

Hi. I have a booking for later this month. Please can you let me know what we should do when we arrive? Thanks

Reply

Thank you for booking with Sentinel Car Park.

Your Arrival
Simply check in at reception and leave the rest to us. The car park is ½ mile from the terminal building. One of our FREE courtesy buses will take you and your luggage to the airport immediately – transfer time approx. 2 minutes.

On your return
We will meet you directly outside the arrivals hall, no phone call necessary. Your car will be ready and waiting at SENTINEL for you to drive away.

Dear Ms Smith

Thank you for your booking made over the telephone yesterday. I can confirm receipt of your deposit of £125.00.

You have booked our property reference Cras 013 from 4 to 11 May next year and your balance of £375.00 will become due 8 weeks before your arrival date.

Thank you again for booking with us. We hope you will enjoy your holiday.

Yours sincerely

▲ Figure 3.18 Customer service by e-mail

◄ Figure 3.19 A letter of confirmation

Have a Go

Know and understand	Apply what you know	Investigate

1 Explain why the hotel receptionist in Figure 3.17 has done her job well.	**2** Practise customer-service role plays:
	
	a as a travel consultant booking a holiday
	
	b as a fitness instructor showing a potential customer around part of a health club
		3 a Either:
		  i Observe a leisure and tourism staff member delivering customer service.
		Or:
		  ii Observe another student in a customer-service role-play.
		
		b Evaluate the strengths and weaknesses of what you see.

Chapter

3.3

Customer complaints and records

Handling complaints

When leisure and tourism employees handle customer complaints, it is important that they listen carefully and are clear about what the problem is. To do this they must stay calm. Leisure and tourism organisations have customer-complaints procedures that staff should follow. The procedures help employees to keep calm because they allow the member of staff to step back from taking the complaint personally.

Leisure and tourism organisation employees know when to refer a customer to a manager or more senior member of staff. This happens when they cannot deal with an issue themselves. All leisure and tourism organisations receive some customer complaints, even if they are minor. Sometimes complaints may be unfair — the customer is not always right. But some complaints are justified. Leisure and tourism organisations want customers to be satisfied and feel that their complaint has been properly handled. They may still bring repeat business and give favourable reports to other potential customers.

If necessary, customers can threaten to take a leisure and tourism organisation to court. An outbound holiday is an expensive purchase and a dissatisfied customer may want some or all of the money refunded. Tour operators can offer partial compensation to customers with a genuine grievance in the hope that this will satisfy them.

It can be dangerous to walk around visitor attractions such as historic sites. Customers could suffer minor injuries by stumbling on the spiral stone staircases in a castle, for example. The attraction's management may offer compensation if a customer complains. This is a lesser evil than the bad publicity that would follow if the story appeared in the media.

Complaints can be made be in writing, by telephone, e-mail or fax. They can also be voiced face to face. People with jobs in leisure and tourism need to know how to deal with complaints that are expressed by any of these means. They are taught when to ask for help and whom to approach for guidance.

Dealing with customer complaints involves:

- listening carefully to the customer — being polite and understanding their problem accurately
- apologising courteously for any inconvenience caused, without yet admitting that the organisation is in the wrong, because some complaints are not justified
- assuring the customer that the issue will be properly investigated and any mistakes corrected
- placing yourself in the customer's position to try to see the problem from their point of view (empathy)
- staying calm, not taking the complaint personally and certainly not arguing with what the customer says
- knowing whether this is an issue you can solve or whether you should bring in a more senior colleague
- trying to solve the problem, if appropriate, and agreeing a way forward with the customer
- making sure that promised responses are actually made and that the customer is aware of any action taken

CaseStudy Face to face at a bowling alley

The customer service given by the bowling-alley employee (in Figure 3.20 on the next page) in response to a problem with a booking had strengths and weaknesses.

Strengths

The employee was polite and gave the customer accurate information. An offer of a café voucher for soft drinks while waiting for a lane to become available was sufficient to satisfy the customer. This would cost the bowling alley little money. Leisure and tourism organisations do not encourage staff to make overgenerous offers to customers at the first signs of a problem. Such offers are usually not necessary and are expensive for the organisation. Empathy has been shown because the staff member has put herself in the customer's position.

Weaknesses

The strengths outweigh the weaknesses. It was not made clear what would happen if a lane did not become available soon but the customer did not ask this question. The attendant should know who to contact for further advice if this issue had been raised. A voucher for free refreshments may be appropriate compensation. Free admission to the bowling alley another time would probably be considered excessively generous and could only be authorised by a senior staff member. This may have been necessary if a lane had not become vacant at 3.00 p.m.

Figure 3.20 Face-to-face customer service at a bowling alley

Have a Go

Know and understand	Apply what you know	Investigate
1 Explain why the bowling-alley employee provided good customer service, from her manager's point of view.	**2** With a partner, role-play the handling of complaints: **a** in a restaurant **b** on an aeroplane	**3 a** Investigate how a named leisure and tourism organisation handles complaints. **b** Describe the procedures that staff follow.

Keeping customer records

Leisure and tourism organisations keep customer records. Up-to-date records help organisations to know who their current customers are. Being aware of which market segments they serve means that organisations can go on to plan future target marketing (see Chapter 2.1).

A tour operator keeps records of customers' names, addresses, telephone numbers and e-mail addresses. Information about where and when they have already travelled with the company is also recorded. Figure 3.21 is the front cover of a Canvas Holidays brochure sent through the post. Customers' details are maintained on a database, which includes customers who have been on Canvas Holidays tours, as well as those who are simply on the mailing list. Tour operators and other leisure and tourism organisations exchange mailing lists with each other, with customers' permission. Booking forms, including online versions, ask customers if they are willing to give such permission (Figure 3.22).

▼ ***Figure 3.21 Canvas Holidays brochure***

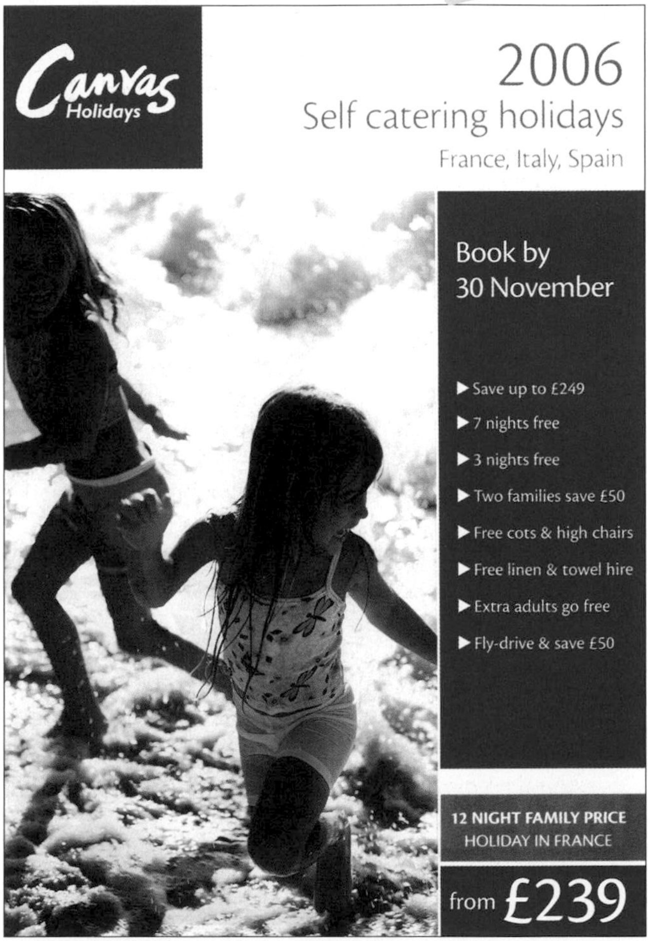

Leisure and tourism employees create and maintain a variety of customer records. Each organisation has its own set of records, which have important marketing roles. For example, customer records can be used for direct marketing (such as sending out flyers and brochures) and for public relations. Some hotels use the records as a Christmas card list, perhaps including details of special spring offers in an accompanying flyer.

Customer records can be stored in paper form or electronically on computers. Whichever system is used, new staff must be shown how to find and change existing customer records accurately. Records of customer details are strictly confidential. Many leisure and tourism organisations are reluctant to show their records to others.

Please tick:

☐ **Yes, I would like to receive details of future offers.**

☐ **by e-mail** ☐ **by post**

▶ ***Figure 3.22 Direct-mail permission request***

A member of staff at a health club has made the record of an answerphone message shown in Figure 3.23. This concerns a problem from the previous evening. KM has passed the message to a colleague. The colleague will need to investigate the customer's complaint and call the customer back. Assuming that the complaint is justified, company policy is to offer an apology and a statement of what action is proposed.

▶ **Figure 3.23**
An answerphone message

Greenbank
Health Club

Answerphone message

From: Mrs Wright

Taken by: KM   **Date and time:** Dec 5 8.20 am

Message: Customer came to swim yesterday after work says two other customers had male children in ladies changing room. Boys too old says customer – should be in male changing room. Says she pointed this out at reception last week but it's still happening.

For action? Yes

Samantha, please see what action was taken after last week's complaint. Check notices about children in changing rooms. Maybe we need new ones? Thanks, K.

Have a Go

Know and understand	Apply what you know	Investigate
1 Make a list of customer records kept by leisure and tourism organisations. Examples in this book are a good start.	**2** Choose one customer record: **a** Complete it. **b** Describe how a named leisure and tourism organisation would use the record.	**3 a** Collect examples of customer records kept by a leisure and tourism organisation. **b** Find out how the organisation uses the records to improve customer service.

Building your customer-service portfolio

Strand by strand

Build up your coursework for Unit 3 ('Customer service in leisure and tourism') by completing one strand at a time. Make each strand a separate section with its own title, starting every one on a fresh page.

Table 3.2 shows the four strands (A–D) that make up Unit 3. The work for each strand is marked separately and your total score for the unit is found by adding up the marks for the four strands. Each strand is marked according to the quality of your work. The marker decides which of three level descriptors matches your work most closely and gives it a mark in that range. Level 1 describes work of the lowest quality and Level 3 is the highest. Table 3.3 shows the level descriptors for Strand A of Unit 3.

A Situations that require staff to have contact with customers and the ways in which one leisure and tourism organisation meets the needs of different types of customers

B Examples of the types of customer records that the leisure and tourism organisation uses and how it deals with complaints

C Details of your dealings with a variety of customers

D Details of your handling of a customer complaint

Level 1	For the chosen organisation, identify situations in which members of staff have to provide customer service and describe, at a basic level, how the needs of a variety of customers are met. *(0–6 marks)*
Level 2	For the chosen organisation, explain clearly why customer service is important and describe, using relevant examples, the ways in which the needs of both internal and external customers are met. *(7–12 marks)*
Level 3	For the chosen organisation, produce a thorough and knowledgeable review of customer service and compare and contrast the way in which the organisation meets the needs of internal and external customers. *(13–18 marks)*

▲ **Table 3.2**
Unit 3 strands

◄ **Table 3.3**
Level descriptors for Unit 3, Strand A

Your work for Unit 3 can be divided as follows (Table 3.4):

- an investigation of the customer service provided by a leisure or tourism organisation
- a record of your involvement in customer service

▶ **Table 3.4**
Dividing Unit 3 into two parts

Part 1	Part 2
Strands A and B	Strands C and D
The same leisure and tourism organisation must be the subject of both Strand A and Strand B	For these strands you can look at the same organisations as for Strands A and B or use different organisations

Your organisation

Strands A and B are based on your investigations into a leisure or tourism organisation. You may use the same organisation for your work in Strands C and D, but this is not compulsory.

The size of your leisure or tourism organisation is important. In Strand A, you must describe ways in which the needs of internal customers are met. Some small leisure and tourism organisations may not give you much scope for this strand. The scale of your organisation should allow you to discover all the information that you need to satisfy the specification requirement. Take advice from your teacher to ensure that your chosen organisation is of a suitable size.

Examples of organisations that you could use are:

- leisure centres
- health clubs
- visitor attractions
- theatres
- museums
- catering outlets
- a home-based leisure facilities (e.g. a DVD/video-rental shop)
- hotels

You can complete the strands of Unit 3 in any order that your teacher agrees, but it is better for assessment to arrange them in the order in which they appear below, and it is advisable to complete Strand C before Strand D. Do not waste time and effort on long, generalised introductions. They will not gain you marks. Get straight on with writing about the customer service in your chosen organisation and then present your record of customer service that you have delivered or simulated.

Strand A

Identify situations in which customer service is provided by your chosen leisure or tourism organisation (Table 3.3). Do this if possible by personal observation and by asking staff in the organisation about such situations. Make sure that you describe clearly and in some detail both internal and external customer service. You should also briefly explain the difference between external and internal customers.

You need to explain why customer service is important for your organisation — why it matters to the organisation as a business. Remember that good customer service generates repeat business and recommendations that lead to more custom. For commercial organisations, this means more profit. Chapter 3.1 supports Strand A.

At Level 3, you need to compare and contrast the ways in which your chosen leisure or tourism organisation meets the needs of internal and external customers. You have to consider both similarities and differences. Similarities include attributes of good customer service, such as politeness, friendliness, efficiency and accuracy. Differences could be the higher priority given to an external customer than an internal colleague when a staff member has to deal with both at once.

Work that is good enough to receive Level 3 marks should include a review of the customer service provided by your chosen leisure or tourism organisation. This review needs to be thorough and to show that you understand in detail how customer service works in the organisation. It is important to note that a *review* is required at this level, not just a descriptive account. Think of book, film or music reviews: they do more than describe what the book, movie or song is about. What makes them reviews is that they give details of strengths and weaknesses — what is done well and what is not, with some idea of how well or how badly. You should take a similar approach in reviewing customer service in your organisation.

Strand B

Table 3.5 lays out the requirements of Strand B. Start by collecting examples of customer records used in your chosen leisure or tourism organisation. For even the most basic mark at Level 1, you need at least two different records. Chapter 3.3 should give you some ideas of what to look for. Leisure and tourism organisations can be protective of customer records since they are confidential. You do not need examples of *completed* customer records — blank ones are enough.

▶ **Table 3.5**
Level descriptors for
Unit 3, Strand B

Level 1	Give at least two examples of customer records used by the organisation and describe, at a basic level, how to assist different customers in a helpful manner. This should include how to deal with complaints and when to direct customers to a supervisor.	
		(0–5 marks)
Level 2	Describe clearly how the organisation deals with complaints and uses customer records, and briefly describe what effect this has on the level of customer service provided by the organisation.	
		(6–10 marks)
Level 3	Explain thoroughly how the organisation deals with complaints and uses customer records, and evaluate what effect this has had on the level of customer service provided by the organisation.	
		(11–14 marks)

In your written work for Strand B, you must describe how to help customers. This can include some general information about what is good practice, but it is better to set it in the context of your organisation. Your description needs to include sections on how to deal with complaints and when to refer situations to a supervisor. Accounts of generalised good practice are valuable here, but it is better to apply what you write to your organisation. How do its employees deal with customer complaints? When do they refer situations to a more senior member of staff?

Leisure and tourism organisations of any size often have staff induction and training programmes. The training materials that they use could be a valuable secondary source of information about the organisation's specific procedures. You can also ask employees about what they do and what is expected of them — primary sources of information.

Find out and report on how your chosen organisation uses the customer records you have collected. Discuss how and to what extent this affects the customer service that is provided there. Ask employees what they think. Talk it over with fellow students and your teacher so that you produce a thorough evaluation. Do not simply include weighed strengths and weaknesses, but also suggest and justify possible improvements. Draw a conclusion about how much each of the records influences the customer service that is provided.

Strand C

This is the first of the two strands that cover your own delivery of customer service. Dealing with complaints is a particular form of customer service that is assessed in Strand D. You should not deal with complaints in Strand C.

Practise customer-service delivery before you are assessed in this task for Unit 3. You can prepare and be assessed equally well in real work and in simulated role-play situations. However, they must clearly be leisure and tourism organisation settings.

A good approach to capitalising on work experience or part-time leisure and tourism employment is to see customer service you provide there as practice from which you can learn skills. Then transfer these skills to role plays that are assessed by your teacher. This works particularly well if you need to transfer customer-service skills from a non-leisure and tourism situation to a true leisure and tourism context.

It is vital that your record of customer service provides objective evidence:

- that you have actually provided customer service (in real or simulated situations)
- of how good the customer service you provided was
- of how your service delivery compares with the descriptor words given in Table 3.6

| **Level 1** Candidates present themselves to the customers appropriately and communicate clearly, both listening carefully and responding appropriately. *(0–3 marks)* |
| **Level 2** Candidates can deal confidently with a variety of customers in a variety of situations, demonstrating good presentation and communication skills. *(4–6 marks)* |
| **Level 3** Candidates can communicate successfully and confidently with customers, listening carefully and providing a full and effective response. *(7–9 marks)* |

◀ *Table 3.6 Level descriptors for Unit 3, Strand C*

Witness statements signed by your teacher are powerful forms of evidence. They should not just certify that you have carried out customer service, but also justify how it compares to the descriptors in the Unit 3 specification. Supporting evidence could include witness statements from your fellow students (peer observation) and self-evaluation that may be based on a transcript. It is important to realise that a transcript alone does not provide proof that actual customer service took place. A transcript, if used, needs to be introduced properly so that it is clear what it represents.

You can provide recorded evidence, on video for instance, of your customer-service delivery, but like other forms of evidence this must be accompanied by reliable witness testimony. Your teacher is the best witness. Photographs can be useful supplementary evidence, especially if they are annotated or captioned.

It is important that your evidence, led by witness statements, matches key words in the assessment descriptors:

- appropriate presentation
- clear and successful communication
- careful listening
- appropriate response (full and successful for high marks)
- confident dealing

You need to show evidence of providing quality customer service in at least three different situations. These do not include the customer-complaint situation for Strand D. Although using one or two more situations can be good practice, doing many more is not beneficial. It is how well you have done, not how many times you have done it, that will score you marks. A range of different situations is best and can be chosen from this list:

- face to face
- presenting (e.g. running a simulated resort representative's welcome meeting)
- by telephone
- by e-mail
- listening to, recording and responding to answerphone messages
- by letter

Strand D

At Levels 1 and 2 (Table 3.7), Strand D is about dealing with a customer complaint and then describing what you did. Your work in this strand must be filed separately from that in Strand C. Strand D deserves its own section with a fresh start, coming clearly after the Strand C evidence in your portfolio.

▶ *Table 3.7*
Level descriptors for
Unit 3, Strand D

Level 1 Candidates deal with a customer complaint with guidance.	*(0–3 marks)*
Level 2 Candidates can describe how to deal with a customer complaint.	*(4–6 marks)*
Level 3 Candidates evaluate their performance in the customer-service situations undertaken, including the handling of complaints made by customers.	*(7–9 marks)*

The same quality of objective evidence as described for Strand C is needed for Strand D. If you are aiming to gain high marks by satisfying the Level 3 descriptor (Table 3.7), you must evaluate all the customer-service situations that you have used for assessment in Strand C and Strand D. Give yourself ratings for each situation using the key words in the assessment descriptors. Score yourself on a five-point scale:

1 = weak

2 = room to improve

3 = satisfactory

4 = some good points

5 = consistently high-quality service provided

Try to be honest and objective, taking into account the comments of others (line manager, teacher, peers). You can use these ratings to inform your evaluation of your own strengths and weaknesses when providing customer service. Add suggestions for improvements and justify them.

Presenting your portfolio

Your Unit 3 coursework should be put together in a slim, soft-backed file or folder. Do not use a bulky ring binder or put each page in a separate plastic wallet.

Your Unit 3 work is entirely separate from that for Unit 2 and should be in a different file. Make sure that each strand is separate too, with its own clear title. Present your work as an A4 document. If you have some larger sheets fold them, but make sure that the reader can open them out easily.

Information about building your portfolio for Unit 2 ('Marketing in leisure and tourism') is given in Chapter 2.4.

Index

A

access   40
accommodation   45, 48, 50, 61
active activity   5
actual selling price   91
advertisements   95, 98, 100
after-sales service   88–89
air cabin crew   71
airlines   44, 49
airports   45, 54
Alton Towers   32, 48
answerphone message   129, 140
Areas of Outstanding Natural Beauty
   (AONBs)   5, 58–60, 62
art galleries   24–27
arts and entertainment   5, 14
audio-tours   24, 27

B

Beaulieu   34
behind-the-scenes services   4
Bisham Abbey   18, 19, 20
Blackpool   89
   Pleasure Beach   28
   Tower   6, 28, 30
Blue Badge guides   46–47, 71
Blue Flag award   57
body language   128
bookshops   38
Bournemouth   57–58
Bowness   59, 63
brands   45, 88
Brighton   89

Bristol Zoo   28, 31
brochures   45, 46, 53
brown road signs   31
Buckerell Lodge Hotel, Exeter
   103–106
Buckingham Palace   30, 34
budget airlines   52, 53, 57
bureaux de change   45
business tourism   34, 43, 50, 53, 80

C

Cadbury World   91, 92–94
Camelot   32
Canvas Holidays   139
car-hire firms   49
catering   6, 25, 29, 31, 36, 48, 61
centres of excellence   18–19
Chatsworth   34, 36–37
Chessington World of Adventures   32
Chester Zoo   28
children's play activities   5, 15, 31, 39
city breaks   53
closed questions   129–130
clubbing   40
coach companies   46, 49, 68
coach drivers   71
coastal areas   56–58
commercial organisations   11, 76, 79,
   116, 123
commercials   95, 100
community centres   10
competition   91, 102, 103, 106
computer games   38

concessions   100
conference facilities   18, 31, 105
conference organiser   71
Countryside Agency   58
Countryside Council for Wales   58
countryside recreation   5, 15, 58–60
credit   91
crossing key components   9–11
Crown Jewels   36
Crystal Palace   18
Cumbria Tourist Board   80–81
curators   23
customer comment/feedback cards   84, 120, 126–127
customer complaints   131–133, 136–138, 144
customer profiling   81–82
customer records   138–140, 143
customers   3, 27, 29, 32, 45, 46, *Chapter 3.1*
    actual   83, 95
    dissatisfied   119, 136
    existing   83
    external   123, 143
    internal   123, 126, 129, 143
    potential   83, 95, 100
    satisfied   126, 131
customer service   45, 72, 116–125
customer-service training   120
customer survey   119
customer types   77

D
Darlington   9–14, 49
database   82, 85
delivering customer service   133–134
demonstrations   96
destinations   44, 47, 51
direct marketing   95, 139
direct selling   46
discounts   91
displays   96
disposable income   80
domestic tourism   51, 56
Dove Cottage   59

Durham   97
DVD/video-rental shops   38, 78, 123

E
e-mail   134
empathy   137
evaluation form   82, 88
Exeter   103–106

F
face-to-face communication   128, 137–138
facility   5
fast pass system   32
ferries   45, 54
ferry companies   49
ferry ports   54
fitness instructor   69, 70
Flamingoland Theme Park and Zoo   85–86
flyers   95, 97, 101
Folio Hotels   105
foot-and-mouth disease   62
footpath erosion   63
foreign currency   45
4 Ps   83, 87
front of house department   124

G
Gala Theatre, Durham   95–100
galleries   18, 23–25, 28
Gallup   83
gender   85
Glenmore Lodge   19
ground-staff   69
guiding services   46

H
Hadrian's Wall   34–36
Hampton Court Palace   34, 36
Hawkshead   64
health clubs   9–10, 70–71, 78, 130
Heritage Coasts   58, 62
historic sites   18, 28, 34–36, 66, 136

holiday homes   61
Holme Pierrepoint   18
home-based leisure   5, 15, *Chapter 1.4*
hospitality   22, 31
hotel   124
hotel receptionist   118, 129, 133
hurricane   96

I

in-bound tourism   37, 51, 56
independent travel   50–51
induction   70, 73
international airports   53
International Passenger Survey   84

J

jobs in leisure and tourism   69–73
Jorvik Viking Centre   28, 30
junk mail   95

K

key components of the leisure industry
   4–8, 66
key components of the travel and
   tourism industry   44–49, 66
Kuoni   81

L

LA Fitness   70, 71
Lake District National Park   59, 62–65,
   80–81
Lake District Tourism and Conservation
   Partnership   64
leaflets   97, 101, 112
LEGOLAND®, Windsor   32, 33–34
leisure activities   2–4
leisure assistants   69
leisure centres   9, 40, 76, 78
leisure facilities   8, 23, 24, 28, 61
leisure industry   *Chapter 1.1*, 23
leisure-time choices   39–41
leisure tourism   43
letter of complaint   131–132
libraries   38

lifeguards   69
Lilleshall   18
limited access   35
litter   62
local leisure customers   49
logos   96, 98, 100
London Eye   28, 30, 49
London Zoo   28
long-haul flights   51–52
Longleat Safari Park   28, 29
Low Wood Hotel, Cumbria   80, 81

M

M6   59
Madame Tussaud's   28, 30
mailshot   95
maintenance department   124
Mallorca   73, 96
marketing   23, *Chapter 2.1*
marketing campaigns   97
marketing mix   76, 83, *Chapter 2.2*, 110
market research   76, 82–85, 87, 112
market segments   77–80, 83, 91, 138
market share   91
merchandising materials   98
methods of travel   53–55
Millennium Stadium   21, 22
MORI   83
motorways   32, 33, 54
mountain centres   19
multiplex cinema   3, 14, 121
multiplier effect   76, 78, 131
museums   11, 18, 23–25, 28
My Travel   73

N

national leisure facilities   *Chapter 1.2*,
   28, 39
national museums   24
National Park Authority (NPA)   59, 63
National Parks   5, 36, 58–59, 62, 69
national recreation centres   78
national restaurant chains   78
National Vocational Qualifications   120

NEC (National Exhibition Centre)   28, 31
Network Rail   123
non-commercial organisations   11, 23, 76, 118
non-English speakers   122
Northumberland National Park   35
Novotel   120
NVQs *see National Vocational Qualifications*

O

objective evidence   146
observation   85
Office of National Statistics   86
online booking   47, 50
online ticket agencies   91
online travel services   47
open questions   129–130
out-bound holidays   51
out-bound tourism   53

P

package holidays   45, 50–51, 53
Palace Pier   28, 30
park rangers   69, 73
passive activity   5
Peak District   36
Pepsi Max Big One   30
personal presentation   130–131
personal qualities   71
personal selling   96
personal surveys   83–84
place   83, 101–102
places of historic interest   60
Plas-y-Brenin   19
Pleasure Beach   28, 30
pollution   62
postal surveys   82–83
posters   98, 101
premiership   20
Pret A Manger   126–127
price   76, 83, 91–94, 102
pricing policy   88, 91, 110–111
product life cycle   89–90, 111
products   3, 24, 32, 36, 83, 102

intangible   89
tangible   88
products and services   12–14, 44, 47, 49, 76, 77, 79, 80, 82, 88, 92, 100, 110, 116, 118
products, services and prices   87–92
promotion   83, 94–101
promotional campaigns   100
promotional materials   77, 94, 97–99, 101
promotional techniques   94, 111
public relations   96, 139

R

Red Cross   100, 102
Register of Exercise Professionals (REPS)   70
repeat business   136
research
    primary   85
    secondary   85
resort representatives   71, 72–73, 89, 96
restaurant managers   69, 119
review   143
role plays   145
roller-coaster   32
Roman Wall   35

S

safari parks   28–29
sales promotions   97
sampling   84
Scarborough   89, 90
seaside resorts   30, 56, 61, 89, 90
services   3, 12–13, 24, 32, 36
short breaks   53
short-haul flights   51–52
signage   92
social groups   80
social impacts of tourism   60–61, 64–65
sources
    primary   39, 106
    secondary   39, 106
South Bank   25–26
special-interest holidays   52–53
special needs   40, 104
Spinnaker Tower   90

sponsorship   96, 97
sport and physical recreation   4, 14
sport spectating   67
sports venues   11, 18, 20–21, 60
staff induction   144
stately homes   29
Stonehenge   34, 35, 49
sustainable management   35, 58, 60
sustainable tourism   62–65
SWOT analysis   76, 87, *Chapter 2.3*, 106, 109, 113

T
take-away restaurants   38, 102
target market   33, 76, 112
target marketing   77–80, 87, 138
Tate Britain   25
Tate Gallery   25
Tate Modern   25–27
techniques   94
technology   45
telephone questionnaires   83
theme parks   18, 28, 32–34, 41, 60, 66
Thorpe Park   32
tourism   28, 43, 67
    economic impacts of   61, 62–63
    environmental impacts of   61–62, 63–64
    impacts of   35, 60–62
    negative impacts of   60–62
    positive impacts of   60–62
tourism jobs   61, 62, 64
tourism types   63
tourist attractions   18
tourist customers   49
tourist guides   71
tourist information centres (TICs)   46, 49, 68
tourist towns and cities   61
tour operators   44, 45–46, 50, 53, 71, 73, 78, 81, 82, 84, 96, 100, 136, 139
    brochures   50
Tower of London   34, 36
town guides   48

training   73, 144
train operators   44, 49
transfer   45
transferable skills   133
Transpennine Express   121
transportation   49, 50
transport providers   44
transport routes   57
travel agents   44–45, 46, 49, 50, 71, 76, 78
travel and tourism facilities   48, 49
travel and tourism industry
    Chapter 1.5
travel brochures   81
travel consultants   45, 71
types of facilities   6

U
UK tourist destinations   48, *Chapter 1.6*
uniforms   130

V
Viewdata   45
village hall   97
visiting friends or relatives (VFR)   43
visitor attractions   6, 15, 23, *Chapter 1.3*, 38, 48, 66, 74, 85, 92, 99, 136
visitor numbers   62

W
welcome meetings   72
'white-knuckle' ride   32, 41, 85
Windermere   59
witness statements   145
Woburn Safari Park   28, 29
work-experience   133, 145
written communication   131–132

Y
Yorkshire Tourist Board   86
Youth Hostels Association (YHA)   64

Z
zoos   28–29, 31